"*The process of prayer –* ⌐ ⌐ ⌐ ⌐ *e drink deeply at that nev* ⌐ ⌐ ⌐ ⌐ *Christian. Yet I have nev* ⌐ ⌐ ⌐ ⌐ *With immense self-awaren* ⌐ ⌐ ⌐ *offers profound insight here for particular people – introverts – whose concerns and contributions are seldom identified yet widely experienced. The whole Church has much to learn here as it seeks to be conformed to Christ.*"

Justin Welby, Archbishop of Canterbury

"*Mark Tanner is an insightful and thoughtful man with a great deal of experience both in theological training and growing churches. This book encapsulates his wisdom.*"

Nicky Gumbel

"*As an extrovert I have found this book incredibly insightful and brilliantly challenging. I will be recommending it to students and younger leaders as a must-read so that we can grow and shape a much more self-aware and generous church family. We need both introverts and extroverts to bring their lives into the communal space we share and we will be a healthier family for it.*

"*This book has challenged me to the core. It has made me reassess how I lead and how I love others. Even now I can think of ways my own church community can be a much more inclusive and releasing space for both introverts, extroverts and indeed every mixture of our God-given humanity. This is an important work and I am grateful to have read it at the start of my leadership journey.*"

Miriam Swaffield, Student Mission Developer, Fusion

"The wonderful message of Pentecost is the pouring out of the Holy Spirit on all people, whatever their gender, age or ethnic background. In this important book, Mark Tanner shows how the personality that we are created to be is included in that universal pouring out. It is a book which demonstrates the maturity of the Charismatic Movement from one of its wisest and most influential leaders."

David Wilkinson, Principal, St John's College, Durham University

"A really helpful book that raises important issues, concerns and questions. Drawn from real life experiences, deep reflection and thoughtful consideration, readers, be they extrovert or introvert, will glean many insights, help and encouragement in their own lives and in understanding and relating to others. A good, accessible read and valuable resource for all personality types and not just those who find themselves in charismatic circles."

Roy Searle, leader, Northumbria Community and former President of the Baptist Union of Great Britain

The Introvert Charismatic

The gift of introversion in a noisy church

Mark Tanner

MONARCH
BOOKS
Oxford, UK & Grand Rapids, Michigan, USA

Published by Monarch Books
an imprint of
Lion Hudson plc
Wilkinson House, Jordan Hill Road,
Oxford OX2 8DR, England
Email: monarch@lionhudson.com
www.lionhudson.com/monarch

ISBN 978 0 85721 588 8
e-ISBN 978 0 85721 589 5

First edition 2015

Acknowledgments
Contributions from correspondents used with their permission and the author's
gratitude.
Every effort has been made to trace copyright holders and to obtain permission for
the use of copyright material. The publisher apologizes for any errors or omissions
and would be grateful to be notified of any corrections that should be incorporated
in future reprints of this book.
Unless otherwise indicated, Scripture quotations taken from The Holy Bible, New
International Version Anglicised. Copyright © 1979, 1984, 2011 Biblica, formerly
International Bible Society. All rights reserved. Anglicised edition first published
in Great Britain 1979 by Hodder & Stoughton, an Hachette UK company. Scripture
quotations marked ESV are from The Holy Bible, English Standard Version® (ESV®)
copyright © 2001 by Crossway, a publishing ministry of Good News Publishers. All
rights reserved. Scripture quotations marked RSV are from The Revised Standard
Version of the Bible copyright © 1346, 1952 and 1971 by the Division of Christian
Education of the National Council of Churches in the USA. Used by permission.
All Rights Reserved. Scripture quotations marked NRSV are from The New Revised
Standard Version of the Bible copyright © 1989 by the Division of Christian
Education of the National Council of Churches in the USA. Used by permission.
All Rights Reserved. Scripture taken from The Message copyright © by Eugene H.
Peterson 1993, 1994, 1995, 1996, 2000, 2001, 2002. Used by permission of NavPress
Publishing Group.

A catalogue record for this book is available from the British Library

Printed and bound in the UK, May 2016, LH26

This book is dedicated to you...

... to the many precious "you"s without whom I would never have found the freedom to do the being behind the thinking behind the writing: most particularly my beloved Lindsay, Jonathan and Pippa

... to you who will read this and through it explore the gift of freedom

... and most of all to You in whom all of this is merely chatter around the edge of the glorious liberty You invite us into in Your Son and by Your Spirit.

Contents

Foreword

The charismatic movement is perhaps the most significant movement in the history of the church in the twentieth century and the beginning of the twenty-first century. The charismatic revival in the mainstream churches, the development of house churches which led into a variety of different charismatic streams, the rediscovery of signs and wonders, and the worldwide amazing growth of Pentecostalism has shaped worship, theology, ecumenism, discipleship, and mission. It has shaken the foundations of and renewed the main denominations and opened up the space for new churches and networks.

Yet all new movements carry with them implicit caricatures which are used by opponents to attack, and by adherents to give identity. The early Methodist revival was criticized for its emphasis on enthusiasm which was seen as dangerous to the social order. To claim that someone is a charismatic has a similar caricature: that of an extrovert enthusiast.

A few years ago during a Methodist Communion service I approached a woman and held out my hand to share the peace with her. She responded, "No, thank you. I don't do that sort of thing." And then she added, "I hope you aren't one of that happy-clappy tongue-speaking lot." For her, extrovert Christianity was coupled with a certain type of music, worship, strangeness in behaviour, and personality.

Such caricatures do a disservice to a movement which has always had diversity but has increasingly matured and become self-reflective in recent decades. Perhaps more importantly, it presents the danger that people from outside the movement will hide behind the caricature and people within the movement will feel squeezed into a mould that denies who God wants them to be.

As someone who has grown up as a Christian within charismatic circles, I am therefore enormously grateful for this book by my friend and colleague Mark Tanner. From rich and diverse experience at the heart of the charismatic movement, embedded in leadership of a local parish church, national networks, and theological education, he explores the real enthusiasm of the introvert charismatic. With honesty and humour he gives us the biblically grounded resources by which all people can grow maturity in Christ and live in the power of the Spirit.

This is significant for a number of reasons. First, it is an encouragement and challenge to those who are introverts, to value their personality in growing in holiness. Second, it is an encouragement and challenge to the already diverse charismatic movement to value and create structures which learn from and work for all. Third, the book is a key demonstration of the humility, confidence, and strength of today's charismatic leaders which enables difficult but ultimately fruitful questions.

The truth is that I have some sympathy for the woman who would not rather share the peace with me. She in fact greeted me generously after the service and we got to know each other reasonably well. She needed permission to be different and the space not to conform in a way that denied who she really was. It is only in recognizing true difference that we can grow together in the unity of the Lord Jesus Christ. As a young Christian I hated those moments when we were instructed to hold hands and sing "Bind us together"! I just wish I had had the resources of this book for moments like that.

Revd Professor David Wilkinson
Principal, St John's College, Durham University

Preface

There is nothing more profoundly fulfilling than experiencing the Lord moving by His Spirit and touching people's lives in great grace and remarkable power. This is, quite literally, what we were made for. In the fullness of God's work is the fullness of life for which we were created. I believe that His kingdom is coming and that we are invited into the adventure of participating in that break-in as God reclaims, redeems, and recreates. This is the stuff of grace: God's grace in action. His *"charis"*, to use the original New Testament word for "grace", is at work and this "charis-matic" experience is very good.

The trouble, at least for me, is that the UK church, of which I am part, has largely bought into the myth that to be "charismatic" you must be extrovert in your character and action. Much teaching has been adopted unreflectively and uncritically from the United States, home in generalized terms to a precious but far more outgoing culture than our more reserved British one. We accept it gladly because we are hungry for the goodness of God to be more clearly evident among us and we see something of what we want in confident US preaching and large churches. In our ravenous haste, however, we appear to assume that we need to shout to make God move in power.

For many of us, especially those who are more introvert in

personality, this means that we are in an uncomfortable place where charismatic culture can seem shallow, loud, driven, and insensitive, but where we love the stuff that God is doing. What is going on? Is introversion a sin to be forgiven, an illness to be healed, or some kind of oppression to be defeated?

I have come to believe that introversion is none of those things. It is a creation gift. It is part of the image of God. Just as man is not woman and woman is not man, but relating together they reflect the fullest expression of the image of God, so it is with introvert and extrovert. Neither is more right (or more wrong) than the other. Each needs the other, and only together can a full expression of the kingdom be explored. God created us to live in covenant community with each other and with Him, and chose to do so by creating us each as unique creations, different to each other but belonging to each other. This difference, when lived in love, releases life, joy, and creativity, as we reflect in our shared human identity something of the diversity of the creator. However, we are fallen as well as created, and difference intended to reflect the creator is so easily distorted by sin into oppression and control.[1]

The question, though, is "How?" How do we live this? How do we share this? How do we not use the difficulties that difference throws up as excuses to wimp out of the challenges with which God would face us? "Hey, don't look at me – I'm an introvert!" is not a "get out of jail free" card that can be played just because we are uncomfortable. How, conversely, do we release the gifts that introverts bring and share them with a hungry church and a dying world? It is these questions that this book sets out to address.

This work arises out of a person, a life, a walk with the Lord, and a pair of eyes that are at least occasionally and partially open. It is not a particularly academic work. It is not a defence of one way of being a Christian or an attack on others. It is not a magic way to be a better disciple or an analysis of previous failure. It is a reflection on the road that I have been created to walk with the Lord arising from the dawning realization that I was not made by mistake.

My hope in writing is fourfold:

I write, firstly, because I want to inhabit the glorious liberty of the children of God in and through the person that God has made me. Why do I put it like that? For the simple reason that if I can't explore something as I am then I can't ever really know it: I will never be anyone else. It's an old saying, but nevertheless true, that "If you're not yourself then you're nobody." This must be taken with a big theological caveat: I am a sinner, albeit a redeemed sinner, and I am being sanctified daily by the work of God in me. I am a new creation in Christ; the old has gone and the new has come. I know this, but my point here is otherwise. I have been created and that creation bears certain hallmarks. I have two feet, I am male, and I am an introvert. I need to use my all that I am for the Lord. My maleness needs to be in the service of Christ, my feet should serve the kingdom (I'm not joking: "How beautiful on the mountains are the feet of those who brings good news", Isaiah 52:7), and I also need to learn to worship and serve as an introvert. Conversion to Christ didn't give me an extra foot, or turn me into a girl, and it does not make me an extrovert.

My hope, secondly, is that this will be helpful for others who find themselves in a similar position to me, apparently facing a choice between walking with the Lord as themselves or following Him as He does remarkable things in the here and now. As I put this in black and white the nonsense of that dichotomy is plainly apparent, but for many of us, much of the time this is the choice which we feel we face. This need not be, and I pray that this book might be the start of something new for many; the start of a journey of authenticity and freedom which brings life to many, for when the sons and daughters of God find life in who they are called and created to be then the kingdom of God has come a step closer.

Thirdly, I hope that in writing this we might gain a fuller and clearer picture of the kingdom. If I am right in my assertion that the introvert/extrovert tension is a blessed part of the created order then it is logical that we only find fullness in the living of that tension. Introverts, though, are not always brilliant at being in dialogue, particularly in high-energy verbose settings such as the world of the renewed churches. We process things internally rather than in the "cut and thrust" of debate and we don't usually push our ideas forward, not least because we don't need to. This struck me forcefully on one occasion when I was in a senior leaders' meeting and was surprised at someone bemoaning the fact that some people would not put themselves forward for "up front" things, which meant that those in leadership needed telepathic gifts to discern who would like to do what. I understood what was meant, but it clashed with numerous assumptions that I realized I made. Firstly, I tend to locate some types of discernment in more private, reflective conversations rather than group discussion. Secondly, I tend to think that people need time to ponder before volunteering. Thirdly, in my roles as pastor in different contexts, I have often observed that when you volunteer you make yourself vulnerable to rejection, which causes pain. I realized I had assumed people would prefer to do that quietly. So, in one comment in a long meeting the lid was taken off two quite conflicting approaches to leadership. One might resemble the bustle of a marketplace, the other the networked interaction of a monastery: one gave people the chance to "have a go"; the other encouraged people to develop through reflective engagement. Is either inherently better? I don't think so… but the models do clash. We need both in healthy operation, and we must be alert to the resulting tension in order that it might be creative and life-giving.

Finally, I hope that this work might give some of our extrovert siblings something of an insight into the other half[2] of the world. I believe that introverts are a blessing to the world and to the church, but unless we learn to express this we will not be able to offer the gifts that we bring. I am most definitely not saying that introverts are better than extroverts, and if you ever think I am implying that then please forgive me and discard that thought, but we do have much to offer. In this, and in a number of the strands of my thinking here I am indebted to Adam McHugh for his excellent book *Introverts in the Church*. This work differs from his in that it expresses questions in the specific context of the renewed part of the British church, as indeed his work does in the wider context of American evangelicalism. I contend that this is vital because it is about the authenticity of what those of us who have been shaped by the UK church have to offer. Together we are, by and large, a more reserved people, particularly when compared with our US cousins. That is not a weakness and neither does it make us superior, however we may feel when we face a classic stereotype like an apparently over-confident or unnecessarily cheery American. It is simply a part of who we are. The question is how we inhabit our own identity and offer praise to God, and together we can learn from the experience of the introvert among us.

I offer this reflection, then, as a gift to the people of God. May it be a sacrifice of praise, an expression of worship as we explore more of the wonderfully diverse creation of our amazing God. May it be a gift of freedom and a revelation of community. May it be a blessing.

1

An Introduction

I t was a Thursday evening in the summer of 2010 and a group of friends were sitting around in comfortable chairs in the middle of what looked like a building site. In two days the New Wine Summer Conference[1] would begin and we were the team with oversight and responsibility for the event. We had run these weeks together before, the planning was done, we knew each other well, and the mood was relaxed and excited as the conversation flowed.

One of the team leaned back in her chair and out of nowhere came out with an off-the-cuff observation which opened up something I had often sensed but never fully explored: "I do feel sorry for introverts at times like this…"

My response was unprocessed and instantaneous, and I'm not sure which caused more shock – the comment or my response, "Not half as sorry as we feel for extroverts!", whereupon a number of things were evident.

Roughly half the group were sitting forward in friendly animation in response to the first comment. In an atmosphere of trusting, warm, but nonetheless serious banter people were saying things like:

"You can't say that!!"

"I'm an introvert and I love this week!"

At the same time, though, my friend who had made the original comment was sitting with her mouth wide open and a look of utter astonishment on her face. I can't remember the exact words, but the question was how I could possibly feel sorry for an extrovert. The conversation was animated and impossible to reproduce exactly, but I attempt to give the sense of it below. Around half the group would self-identify as introvert, and half as extrovert, although I suspect that many of us would be what Susan Cain might call "ambivert".[2] We talked at length, with different people representing the "camps" at any one time, and the conversation felt something like this:

> Extrovert: But this week is heaven for extroverts, and must be a nightmare if you need space! There are thousands of people camping together, with large meetings, enthusiastic worship, and loads of people to talk to all the time.

> Introvert: You're right that it is tiring for those of us who are introvert, but we still need and want the stuff that this week offers. We need friends, and teaching, and encouragement, and prayer, and all that this week offers. We look forward to all that we get from events like this.

> Extrovert: But isn't it oppressive to be with people all the time if you are introvert?

> Introvert: That is the world we live in all the time. We learn to deal with it. We need space to recharge our batteries. Time alone or in intimate

conversation is rich and precious to us and you can make that anywhere; even here.

Extrovert: And how can you get space in a week like this? I am on the go all the time.

Introvert: You're "on the go" because you are extrovert. In reality being in a crowd can be one of the best places to be alone. Have you noticed how, when we are together in the main meeting, it will sometimes take me a while to catch on if we are all told to do something? It might look like I am not listening, but to me it's like everyone else is being looked after so I can just focus on God. Once I learned that I didn't have to do what everyone else was doing it became like it's just me and Jesus in the room.

Extrovert: I can see that…

Introvert: And while you are in the middle of a crowd of new folk all talking energetically, I will often be in a quiet conversation with someone. It might be an old friend or someone new…

Extrovert: … actually you are really good at that. You notice when there is someone who is not comfortable, or who is hanging back, and you are the one who can get alongside them.

Introvert: Sometimes… although it doesn't always feel like that.

Extrovert: No – you're good with people. In fact I'm not sure that you are really an introvert at all. You lead big meetings, you run a big church, you speak in public all the time – people like you!

Introvert: None of those things make you extrovert, though. It's easy to lead or speak "up front" if you are good at it, and some of those leaders will be introvert, others extrovert. Introversion is about where you get energy... so I really envy the way you can effortlessly come up with conversation and banter and keep up with people. You make it look so easy whereas I always have to work at it.

Extrovert: I guess it's easier if you're an extrovert and so you're not shy...

Someone: ... but none of us in this room is exactly shy.

Extrovert: How can you say you are introvert if you are not shy?

The group: No, no, no... being an introvert and being shy is not the same thing. Introverts get energy from being alone or being with few others; extroverts get energy from being with others.

Introvert: I don't often feel shy, but I do find that after a while I just feel exhausted of being with people and just want to find some space.

Extrovert: But how can you say that you feel sorry for extroverts?

Introvert: Aha! Because we all need time with other Christians and we all need time alone with God. Both are vital if we are going to be healthy Christians. If we are always with others we will never face deep truths about ourselves or spend time just focusing on the Lord. If we are always by ourselves we develop faith that is in danger of being entirely self-referential and in our own image, as well as growing stagnant and detached from reality.

Extrovert: So why does that make you sorry for us?

Introvert: Because introverts are pretty much forced to spend time with others and in weeks like this we get loads of great input, but something inside always draws us back to the quiet place. My favourite time of the day is the very early morning when no one else is up and I can be alone with a cup of tea, the Bible, and Jesus.

Extroverts need time alone with God just as much, except they are not drawn to it by something inside themselves in the same way, and no one else is going to take them by the hand and drag them there.

Extrovert: But I love this week – it is one of the most important weeks of my year.

Introvert: And so do I… but I recognize that while you can take me with you to the riches you naturally gain from a conference like this, actually I can't easily take you to the precious quiet place that is so essential to spiritual health. You won't be able to help yourself dragging me with you... and nine times out of ten that is wonderful, but I can only find my natural habitat by withdrawing sometimes, and I can't really do that for you.

Extrovert: I can see that... but I am still glad to be extrovert!

Introvert: And I am glad you are too... but I still feel a little sorry for you!

We will return to what we really mean by the words "introvert" and "extrovert", where these terms come from, and why they are useful. This is something that affects each of us deeply, and yet we rarely discuss it. This is beginning to change, not least with the work of Susan Cain and Adam McHugh, but I still find that I am introducing people to the area every time I teach about it. As we talk it is as if people are being given permission to be themselves, and this is vital if we are truly to be the people God created us to be.

There is much unseen bunkum around in the Christian world that arises from our tendency to take culture and cultural assumptions on board along with the truths that really are universal about Christ and the good news of the kingdom. We hear and accept the gospel and unconsciously adopt the characteristics of those who brought it to us. We feel that to "worship properly" we need to dress a certain way, talk with certain words, behave in a particular fashion, and do particular things with our bodies. We can mock this where we see it, but all of us know the pressure to raise our hands, or kneel at a certain point, or clap, or not clap, or cross ourselves or definitely not to scratch our nose in case people think we are crossing ourselves... or to behave in an extrovert way.

It is hard to examine deeply inbuilt cultural assumptions, such as "the extrovert ideal" that Cain describes as fundamental to evangelical Christianity, despite extroversion being entirely inessential to the basic message of Christ. As I have talked with numerous people about this over the last few years it is both astonishing and delightful to see people grasp the simple truth that introversion is a deeply precious gift which they, we, are invited to inhabit fully, freely, and generously.

I think of the first seminar I offered on this subject, after which I had a queue of people waiting to talk with me. I reflected later that I had never been mobbed so quietly by so many people. Person after person took my hand, looked me in the eye, and simply said "thank you". One man told me that the session felt to him like I had installed a camera in his house and spoken about what I had seen over the last few years.

The seminar simply shared some basic insights about being an introvert, drawn from widely available material we shall look at later, and then shared some reflections on being an introvert Christian. There is no rocket science here, but there is huge value in discovering the freedom to be who we were made to be.

Conversely, I recall a young lady who was speaking in a large meeting. She had been to a session exploring this area, and when describing it she observed with great excitement that she was an extrovert but there were introvert Christians too. She told us that "they" are the kind of people you see sitting by themselves reading, maybe in the café or the bar. Then she said, and I quote, "I never realized they were introvert; I thought they just had no friends."

The main thing I have noticed, though, is that this area

unlocks a lot of quiet guilt and even a sense of fear. As I talk with groups and individuals one clearly recurring theme is that people worry that they are missing out because they are the type of person that they are. Later I will make the case that God has deliberately made us different and needing each other in order to open to us the blessing of genuine fellowship and cooperation. Male needs female, left needs right, introvert needs extrovert, and vice versa. Not all of these are mutually exclusive categories, either: this is not about pigeonholing or limiting people. It is about interdependence, valuing the other, and learning to be the body of Christ within which none of us has everything. We all bring something. God's people belong together and need each other. However, despite knowing this in theory, we tend towards functional blindness to this truth, and so many of us yearn for self-sufficiency.

So as we talk about being introvert and yet being a lively Christian engaged in ministry and mission, many extroverts, who feel the need to process verbally what has been said, will describe feelings of guilt that they are not better at prayer or contemplation. They will often speak of frustration that they "cannot do silence", and confess that they get bored reading the Bible or trying to pray.

Conversely, I have been party to many quiet conversations with introvert Christians who value space but feel that they are missing out on the more enthusiastic side of faith. There is longing expressed to be able to "join in enthusiastically", and yet an inner integrity knows that this is not an authentic expression of the encounter that they are having in that moment with God. Others seem to be drawn to the place of exuberance, and that is lovely, but for them there is a reserve that is precious but leaves questions of whether they have missed out, whether they could have "tried" harder or responded differently.

I comment on this carefully because these conversations are deeply precious. There is something holy about glimpsing God at work in conversation with His children. God does invite people into fuller engagement with Him, but this invitation comes to the people we are, not to the people we would like to be. It is important to note these feelings of guilt or failure but also to grasp that this is a place from which we are invited to journey: it is the start, not the end, of a process. Clearly we are called to engage with God in ways that go beyond our preferences, but the extrovert should not feel guilty that they find silence hard. The question is how they learn to do intimacy and solitude with God as an extrovert, not whether they are "faulty" in some way. Similarly, and we shall come to some resources for this later, how do we introverts best engage with the body of Christ, fully and completely, but still authentically? What God holds out in Christ is invitation rather than condemnation, the conviction that we can move forward with Him, not imprisonment in our failure.

Please notice this as we journey together around this subject. Conviction is good! Condemnation is bad! Conviction occurs when the Spirit of God whispers in your ear that you are not where you should be before God and holds a hand of grace out in order that you might move, change, repent, or grow, and live in line with His good and perfect will. Conviction leads to hope and freedom. It may not be comfortable, but has good fruit. You may well be convicted as you read this, and such conviction should be heeded.

Condemnation, on the other hand, comes from elsewhere. It can, at first, sound like conviction, except that it tends to leave us feeling empty. Whereas conviction is an invitation, condemnation is an accusation that drives us away from hope. Such condemnation does not belong to those who are in Christ.

Its fruit is despair and hopelessness, denial and self-loathing. It is a whispering voice that tells us that we are no good and we will always fail to live up to what Christ invites us to. Our personality type does not condemn us; God is bigger than we can imagine and character is a gift.

Meanwhile, back with the New Wine team: we have returned to this question of introversion within an explicitly charismatic movement in conversation and seminars. The opportunity arose for a new team to lead a new quiet prayer venue at one of the summer conferences. I was encouraged to convene a group and ask what we could provide which would nurture, encourage, and bless delegates of a more introvert personality type. Roger Preece, an Anglican vicar and friend of mine, has taken the lead as we have worked with a team of ordinands from Cranmer Hall and created something remarkable...

An oasis of gentle, rhythmic quiet spaciousness in the middle of a wonderfully boisterous and enthusiastic gathering of Christians who don't always explicitly exude the charism (or spiritual gift) of calm or peace. Despite being in a cowshed and able to hear the bustle of the young people's venues, delegates step through the door, remove their shoes, and inhabit a beautiful and calm space which the team create in which they can engage with God. Some lie on the floor; others write. Some paint; others sit and read the Scriptures. Many gather for simple, quiet, liturgical prayer slots throughout the day in which it is easy to understand what was expected.

In the evenings this venue has sometimes been open as an alternative to the main meeting, with the talk being relayed by radio link from the large gathering, but set in the context of reflective worship. Paradoxically we have found that this "spacious venue" became overcrowded in the evenings as people looked for teaching set in the context of peace and rhythm.

I talked with the leaders and asked what kind of things people were saying about the venue having experienced it. These are some of the comments:

> "This is a place of balance."

> "I can withdraw here."

> "I feel able to recharge and reconnect with God."

> "Peace" is a word that was connected a lot to the sense of encounter people had in Sanctuary.

> "[Here] there is more space."

The appetite for this kind of provision is great, but what is it that we are looking to encourage and nurture? What is it to be introvert? What is it to be an introvert evangelical or, even more difficult to comprehend, an introvert charismatic?

It's time that we thought more carefully about the concept of introversion, and then we will consider what we mean by charismatic and how we might engage as introverts in an extrovert church. A couple of notes will help you understand the shape of this book and how you might use it. The numbered chapters develop the flow of the work from beginning to end. They are "interrupted" by short pieces entitled "meet *someone*" which introduce you to various other people with whom I have conducted structured conversation about this area. This is not a theoretical book, nor one which is trying to pigeonhole people. It is a description of part of the real world with wild and glorious difference and some helpful insights. In meeting other introvert charismatics I hope that we can limit the danger of stereotyping or building lazy conformity. We have so much to learn from our introvert charismatic siblings (which is a word I use meaning "brothers and sisters" to try to be inclusive).

You will also find two letters written to introverts and charismatics. This is a different way of exploring the personal dynamic of this subject. We are talking about real lives of real people. What we are exploring rises from our common experience as we live in the complex and glorious image of God.

So let's explore!

2

What is an Introvert?

I have been using the term "introvert" as if we have agreed what we mean by it. There has been much popular interest in this topic over the last few years, meaning that many of us are familiar with the term. The danger, though, is that we understand different things from the same word, so let me be clear what I am meaning when I use it.

I am using the term in the way that the Myers-Briggs Personality Type Indicator (MBTI) course does. You may well know about this popular psychological tool for describing personality; it is based on the work of Carl Jung and basically seeks to discern where people stand on four basic divisions it describes within human personalities. To summarize, it will describe you as:

- **Introvert (I) or Extrovert (E)** – which is to do with where you get your energy and gain your insight. We will return to this in a moment.

- **Intuitive (N) or Sensing (S)** – which is to do with how you perceive the world, either in concrete (S) or imaginative (N) terms. The "S" builds on what is known ("this is a table"), whereas the "N" imagines what could be created ("this would make a great den").

- *Thinking (T) or Feeling (F)* – which is to do with how you make decisions or come to judgments, either from a relatively detached rational standpoint (T), or from an empathetic engaged position (F). The "T" analyses; the "F" reacts from the heart.

- *Judging (J) or Perceiving (P)* – which is to do with how we engage with the world, either primarily from a decisive position (J) or one of observation (P). A "J" will get essays or holiday planning done in plenty of time because they like to be secure in the knowledge that everything is in order, whereas a "P" will leave them to the last minute because there is always more to know and more possibilities to be explored.

A person will, of course, have some of all eight of these characteristics, but will tend towards a preference which is demarcated by a four-lettered personality type (like "EFTJ" or "ISFP"). This can be useful when employed as a tool for understanding the self and others; it should be noted that it can also be damaging when it is used lazily and becomes a box into which we squeeze ourselves or anyone else.

This is not a full description, or defence, of MBTI. I find it a useful tool that gives me a language with which to question my personality and preferences and that of those around me. I am wary of a number of aspects of MBTI, not least the idea that we can be neatly pigeonholed or tied down in a perpetual static "type".[1] A wise and self-aware ordained theologian with whom I corresponded in preparation for this book observed:

> I used to think of myself as an extrovert, but as I
> have got older I realize I gain energy in my own
> company as well as with others. That energy is like
> a deep stream to draw from. The energy I get from
> people is more like a babbling brook. It's great but
> lacks the depth I find in being solitary.

People feel like they grow and develop, and of course they do. Whether they change "category" is not important for our thinking here; we are seeking that which is helpful and useful in understanding ourselves and others, not constructing a scientific edifice. Others, particularly Susan Cain in the popular sphere, have written more robust defences of the scientific rationale behind our understanding of introversion; this book is about ideas, approaches, and language that will enable us to engage with God and each other more fully and in a more healthy fashion. We are giving ourselves permission to notice that we gain different things from different environments and that the church is enriched by the different personalities within it.

An introvert is someone who is comfortable in, and gains energy from, the inner world. They deal naturally with ideas, concepts, feelings, or images, and will tend to work with a reconstructed model of the world within themselves. They work well when they have space to reflect, they are often good at conceptualizing, and they will usually work well alone. Various correspondents have defined or described it as:

> "A person who recharges their batteries by spending
> time alone... a person whose primary world is the
> inner world of thoughts and feelings rather than the
> outer world of action and interaction."

"I see my introvert friends as needing much more time to inwardly process things and find a place away from the group where this can be done. The problem is that us extroverts want to keep talking (processing stuff out loud) which means we fill the space. Introverts need decent down-time away from the noise of life to re-energize themselves. Introverts are not necessarily more drawn to one of the five-fold ministries any more than an extrovert but on the whole they seem most comfortable in the ST rather than the APE!"[2]

"The phrase 'introverted charismatic' is interesting. The negative associations I have with both words are significantly mitigated when they are put together. 'Introverted' softens my stereotype of noisy arm-waving loons. 'Charismatic' softens my stereotype of nerdy awkwardness. Put together the words suggest a person of gentleness, stillness, strength, depth, openness to God's Spirit, a person who is quietly observant, notices what God is about – there are connotations of wisdom here."

"Introverts, to me, are people whose subconscious actions and reactions are, more often than not, internal or aimed at the inner life. This may be seen by an overactive internal monologue, a preference for private personal reflection, a desire for conversations with others to be on deep issues or on issues relating to a person's inner life, e.g. identity, spirituality, psychological, etc. Introverts find themselves tired or losing a sense of self-

control after long periods of time in the presence
of a crowd."

"My understanding of an introvert nature is
essentially that of choosing to be resourced
inwardly and by practices which feed the inner
person in a more reflective and less overtly
relational manner."

There are more introverts out there than you might think. A
quick search online brings up countless articles on introversion,
including many lists of characteristics that claim to help readers
recognize whether they are introvert. (See, for example, a recent
article in the *Huffington Post* entitled "23 Signs You're secretly
an Introvert".[3]) Such "signs" include:

- Needing space and time in your own company.

- Picking up on details that others might miss.

- Feeling alone in a crowd or at a social gathering.

- Being seen as intense.

- Listening more than you talk.

- "Friends" asking you to "open up" or "come out of your shell".

- Preferring deep and meaningful conversation to small talk or networking.

- Being more comfortable speaking in front of a large crowd than having to make conversation with them.

- Preferring to develop expertise in one area rather than having a go at everything.

- Tuning out or shutting down after too much activity, and taking time out for solitude after busy social periods.

- A tendency either to being distracted easily or concentrating on one thing while the world is hectic around you.

- Not drawing as much excitement and energy from your surroundings as others appear to.

The response to the *Huffington Post* article and others like it was remarkable: it has sparked countless blogs, tweets, comments, and other discussion, both positive and negative. One blog, called GAWKER,[4] observes that you are probably an extrovert if "You do not justify your social impediments as charming quirks indicative of a secretly brilliant personality", and "Sometimes you do things alone without tweeting 'OHHHH ********, I LOVE TO DO THINGS ALOOOOONE!!!!!!!!! #INTROVERT." I quote this partly because it is funny, but also to remind those of us who are introvert of two important truths that we need to hold in tension as we think about this subject. As we explore introversion our insights will not always be fully understood or widely welcomed. This does not invalidate the exploration; however, in asserting the importance of understanding and valuing introversion we need to guard against self-obsession. Introversion is part of life. It is widely recognized, much misunderstood, and important to reflect upon. It is a valuable and beautiful component of the humanity with which we were created.

It is a common experience for introverts in public jobs to find that friends who are getting to know us struggle to believe that we are introvert. Others seem far more "obviously introvert", and all introverts are different. Some will struggle with issues that others don't even notice. Some will trip over something that does not concern others at all. Being introvert does not make you the same as all other introverts. We vary in every way. However, there are important things that we have in common.

Let's start by dispelling a few myths:

Introverts are not necessarily shy

Some, of course, are, and many would appear to be so in certain situations, but to be an introvert is to be one whose energy comes from within and whose reflection is primarily done in a situation where something can be explored to a significant depth. Thus they will often be thoughtful or reflective people, and they will usually prefer the company of a single person or small group to that of a large group of people. However, they may well possess marvellous social skills.

You will find introverts in every walk of life. Many of the best pastors I know are introvert. They listen carefully and give attention. They love people. They engage in parties and social settings both for business and pleasure. Often it takes careful observation to see who is introvert and who is extrovert in a social setting, but afterwards…

… it will be very clear as the extrovert buzzes about all the people she has met and the new possibilities that have arisen, while the introvert shuts down and seeks out a quiet place to recover. So, commonly, in the car after a party an introvert will be silent while an extrovert will not be able to stop talking.

Introverts are not necessarily antisocial

Again, you will find antisocial introverts, but most of us actually really like people… just not too many of them all at once and all the time! We do find it hard when someone is overly pushy or demanding and gives no space for reflection or respect for another's identity. One of the commonly observed truths about introverts and extroverts is that extroverts need more stimulation and introverts can easily find themselves over-stimulated. Such over-stimulation will not create a healthy response in an introvert, who may or may not manage to hide the pain caused but who will use large amounts of energy in dealing with it. There are people and places where I know that I need to find space to withdraw simply to prevent myself being rude as I defend the psychological space that I need to be me. This is why the toilet and the dog can be the introvert's best friends (one being the only room in the house with a lock on the door and the other needing to be walked daily).

However, most introverts will have good quality friendships and can be very popular people. Their friendships will, it must be said, characteristically be fewer and deeper than their extrovert cousin's, but we all need others.

Introverts are not necessarily arrogant

This is a surprisingly common accusation made against introverts, and there are reasons for this, but arrogance and introversion are very different things.

A friend recalls having a run-in with a teacher at school over careers guidance. She had no idea what she wanted to do "when she grew up" and I guess she was not very talkative about the matter because she had nothing of any particular merit to say. She had plenty to chew over, but nothing concrete to which she could commit and there was no way she was going to move towards making a decision that could affect the rest of her life for the sake of a teacher who clearly had an agenda, which was how the "guidance" felt to her.

She was, however, accused of being arrogant and dismissive. Now, maybe she was; she was a teenager who would have been out of her comfort zone and arrogance is not an unknown feature of late adolescence, but she really couldn't see how she was supposed to act differently.

It was only years later that she saw a different interpretation of the interactions that took place. A teacher who was clearly extrovert, based on wider recollections of him, was genuinely seeking to help the pupils. He ran the careers interview with the fixed paradigm that pupils would be able to talk over their futures and move towards some ideas which they could explore. That is what extroverts do: they process externally. Introverts don't. We reflect and chew over, and one of the things that Adam McHugh notes is that we learn to be cautious about sharing our conclusions until they are robust enough to stand up to public scrutiny.

This, in itself, can cause problems because we will develop an idea or an argument internally until it makes sense and can withstand examination. However, when we then offer the fruit of our labour to others who follow an extrovert processing method in discussion, we find our pearl considered for an instant and then discarded as if it were a thought en route to a greater conclusion. This hurts, and so we learn to be quiet.

Thus, this teenage friend listened diligently and took material to ponder, but needed time to develop and consider. This looked to the extrovert teacher like withdrawal, but would have felt more like consideration to the student. The pupil felt the teacher was invasive, and was in turn perceived as arrogant. Neither assumption was fully true.

Introverts are not necessarily inarticulate

We usually listen more than we talk, but you can't judge an introvert by the quantity of their words. Introverts and extroverts often differ in their adherence to the old adage "think before you speak". To an introvert that is simply what we do; to do otherwise is to be foolish. To demand that of an extrovert, though, is to tell them not to think. They think by speaking and discussing; they "think aloud"; they process with others and draw their energy from a shared life.

This is, however, a useful reminder that we must always remember that we are not exploring an "exact science" in this discussion. I think of a discussion I had with a couple I know well, where the wife is clearly and strongly introvert and the husband equally obviously extrovert. For them, however, she, the introvert, will need to discuss things as her thought process develops because she is also strongly "P" on the Myers-Briggs scale. Thus she comes to a decision late in the process, whereas he, as a "J", decides early and tends towards more decisive statements. Remember that while the discussion in which this book is engaged is useful for understanding and dialogue, it is descriptive rather than prescriptive. The wise reader will contain their developing understanding with sufficient grace and caution to avoid pigeonholing others.

A wise young curate whom I interviewed commented: "I wonder if there could be problems exploring anything connected to personality type and spirituality in that people may pigeonhole themselves and say I am introvert/extrovert therefore I need quiet/loudness when actually we all need both in different combinations at different times."

Introverts are not necessarily self-sufficient...

... although many of us can fall into the trap of believing we are. We were not created to live alone and any introversion/extroversion preference does not deny or diminish this. We naturally process, reflect, and discuss internally and in intimate settings, but we cannot stand alone any more than others can. We are not the only source of wisdom or insight. We may not simply love ourselves. We are creatures of covenant community, but there are times when we need help in realizing this in both senses of that word. (In other words, both in the sense of recognizing it is true and in the sense of making what is theoretically true into a concrete reality.)

A healthy introvert, then, is one with a strong and sustaining internal life. We have discovered that our energy is replenished in the quiet and deep place. We love to reflect and we need to withdraw. We need rhythm to sustain us, and often find that it is only in order and balance that we can survive in the chaotic socially tidal world we inhabit.

We fear the exhaustion that ensues when there is no respite from others, and the flattening experience of being swept along by an extrovert friend or community who, unwittingly and uninvited, will trample freely on holy ground. We are wary of the shallowness and apparent insincerity of the world we are so often invited to inhabit. We often struggle with guilt that we have no more to give, but long for the space to think and to be still.

This means that some things are challenging for us, although other things are correspondingly easier. Evangelism, in particular, can be hard, as we are loath to invade the space of others in ways which we so much despise others doing to us. McHugh is very helpful on this, and I would encourage interested readers to refer to his work.[5] We will return to this question practically later. Silent retreat, on the other hand, can be like heaven once we have got used to the strange experience of being allowed not to talk.

Introverts are not an accident. They, we, have been created by God and find it natural to develop and exercise certain gifts which are essential to the health of the church, community, and society. Such gifts are not exclusive, but they are, perhaps, less hard work for some than for others.

Introverts live deeply and are drawn to wisdom. We wrestle and are not easily satisfied with half-answers. We notice the excluded and seek compassion. We are drawn to the quiet place of prayer and the silent battle of faith. These are gifts the church needs and for which the world longs and to which we will return later.

Meet Anna

Anna (whose name has been changed) is a wise and experienced woman who has been a Christian for many years. She is not in "up-front ministry", although she is very involved in her local church.

She says, "I haven't thought of myself as an introvert in the past as I do regard myself as a 'people person', and am fairly outgoing. But when I've done Myers-Briggs... I came out well into the 'introvert' spectrum – so that has led me to a lot of thought, a growth in understanding, and a revised concept of the word 'introvert'.

"Whereas before I saw an introvert as someone 'turned in on themselves' and not outgoing, not sociable, etc. – now, certainly from an MB point of view anyway – I see myself as an introvert who, although very sociable, and quite gregarious at times, needs time to myself to be resourced for those activities. And a whole lot of things started falling into place – like the number of times I've looked forward to parties/social gatherings – only to arrive and feel out of place and want to retreat, feeling excluded, unwanted, and as if I don't 'belong' somehow. I've learned to cope with this much better by reducing the larger gatherings into one-to-one conversations where I try to really interact meaningfully with one person at a time, rather than being concerned with the bigger picture.

"I certainly function best in relationships when they are one to one, or in small groups. And I don't find it easy to share in a group setting. I don't know whether it's a common trait in the introvert – but I find it much

easier to listen than to share about myself (so having a spiritual director/companion/mentor is quite a challenge!).

"Even in a very happy marriage, I find I often crave the (unfortunately rare!) delight of having the house to myself."

She describes herself as charismatic, but says, "I'm wary of labels as I feel as soon as I attach one too firmly it somehow limits the way God can work in my life, and can be restricting rather than liberating.

"I didn't grow up with any understanding of the charismatic – and didn't encounter any teachings on it until well into adult life. For me it's strongly connected with awareness of the gifts of the Spirit – in all their many and varied aspects – including tongues, prophecy etc. – but much more than that. And those gifts are important to me personally in my walk with God (though I don't think I exercise them enough).

"I guess my definition [of being charismatic] would be something to do with being open to the gifts of the Spirit – but not in a proscriptive way."

Her experience of worshipping in a charismatic environment is interesting. She describes herself as "more comfortable on the sidelines or edges" and says that this is why she enjoys doing things like operating the projection software.

"In informal gatherings if I want to stand or express myself more freely I need to go to the back behind others. When [I get] carried away in worship [I am] more

likely to sit or kneel or hold out hands in front than wave [my] arms above [me]."

She feels that "corporate worship is often a struggle" and describes "feeling a lack of engagement in contrast to those around me. People can get in the way! Especially when I feel I'm being told what I should be feeling or doing..." For her, "intimacy with God [is] far more likely to be experienced on my own rather than corporately." Yet she describes herself as one who "loves singing to God – and that love can overcome my introversion. [I am] unlikely to ever dance, but who knows what God can do..."

3

Introversion in the Bible

ere's a challenge: Where do we find introversion in
the Bible? Different people will give different answers
to this question, but unscientific sampling of widely
available material suggests that there are two basic camps into
which people place themselves (if they take an interest at all).

Some will argue passionately that everyone who is anyone
in the Bible is extrovert. So, for example, Jesus is clearly an
extrovert. He chooses to journey with a large group, invests in
thousands of people, is an eloquent speaker, and is a popular,
well-known figure.

Others, meanwhile, will argue with a rather quieter passion
that the Bible is largely populated with introverts. So, by way of a
second example, Jesus is clearly an introvert. He gets up early to
pray by himself, He invests deeply in a few, He presents clearly
developed ideas, and He would rather walk past a boatload of
friends than join them when He is tired.

The argument could go backward and forward and is not, in
my view, very fruitful because it is not asking the right question.
Modern scholarship has developed what are called reader-
centred approaches to texts which give the reader a way to ask

their own questions of a particular body of writing. Think of those who read the Bible from a feminist or liberation-theology perspective. They will see the text in a very different manner because of the questions that are brought to their reading. This process is perfectly valid, but care needs to be taken with it. A text can "answer" questions which are beyond the intention of the original authors, but caution needs to be exercised in order to shape the investigation in a manner that does not simply read the questioner's presupposition into the original material. Christians believe that the Bible is in some sense the word of God, mediated through human authors but rooted in revelation, which gives us confidence to ask modern questions of an ancient text, but we still need to be careful.

So, introversion and extroversion are not categories that would have been known to, or recognized by, those who penned the Scriptures. At one level asking where the introverts are in the Bible is like asking where the footballers were on the *Titanic*. There will have been those who played football – there may have been some who were good at it – but I am not sure that this is a question many people will have asked and thus the search for the footballing implications of the sinking of a twentieth-century cruise-liner will probably not prove very rewarding.

However, the Bible does have much to say about character and personality. There is rich material that shapes and forms us as we seek to follow God and worship from the heart. It is not neatly ordered and divided into sections for introverts, extroverts, and those who don't know what they are. By their instruction, encouragement, example, and challenge – which is read and received differently by all of us – the authors' concern is to shape character in a manner that is holy. Think, for example, of the "wisdom literature" (Job, Psalms, Ecclesiastes, the Song of Songs, and Proverbs in the main canon) and you see a body of work devoted to shaping us before God.

So, while it's not actually very useful to ask where the introverts are in the Bible, there are two valid and fruitful questions that we will explore in this chapter. We will start off by asking where we see typically introvert behaviour, and I will look briefly at the lives of six characters, two from the Old Testament and four from the New. I notice and regret that all the main characters are male, although I will be asking an interesting question of two women from the New Testament.[1] Then we will ask what lessons the Bible seeks to teach with regard to character. This is an incomplete survey, but one which, I hope, will serve to spark further reflection and deeper study.

Where do we see introvert behaviour in the Bible?

Moses

Moses might seem like an odd person to start with. After all, he led the people through the wilderness, battled with Pharaoh, gave the Law, and led his people for many years. His behaviour is public, and yet he was apparently unwilling to be in this place.

Almost the first action that we see Moses take is the killing of the Egyptian slave-driver (Exodus 2), which is an action he takes having checked he is by himself (verse 12). He does not choose to form a gang, and having acted alone he then flees alone when what he has done is discovered (verse 15).

Chapter 3 sees Moses' first and foundational recorded spiritual experience. This is not in some large worship meeting or mediated through another. Moses is alone. The bush burns. God speaks.

Moreover, when God speaks, Moses is very unwilling to obey. He does not think he will be believed, and even when God shows him the coolest trick on the circuit he does not want to go and show it off. Instead he says that he is hopeless at this kind of thing, and twists God's arm into sending Aaron with him.

This behaviour will be familiar to introverts. It is not simply that Moses is unwilling to put himself in the limelight; it is that he processes all of this by himself, and has no desire to show off what he has discovered. Extrovert behaviour would have convened a gathering or run off to Zipporah to talk about it, telling God that they would get back to Him tomorrow. Moreover, once Moses has worked it out with God, he does not consult with others. There is no half-revelation here that is brought for communal discernment. God has spoken, Moses has heard, and this is how it will be understood.

Looking forward we can see that Moses struggles with feeling he should do everything himself, perhaps a classic introvert failing (Exodus 18). We see that he withdraws with God to restore and realign himself (e.g. Exodus 19 or 33). We see the repeated dynamic of his processing with God and pronouncing their conclusions, none of which guarantees he was actually an introvert, but this is classic introvert behaviour and affirms that God can work with this kind of response.

Elijah

I am thinking of one particular incident in Elijah's life: he has defeated the 400 prophets of Baal on Mount Carmel, and Queen Jezebel, who is as aggressive as she is devoted to Baal, reacts strongly and aggressively. These events are recounted in 1 Kings 18, but I draw our attention to chapter 19 in which we see Elijah's response to Jezebel.

It would be possible to argue that Elijah's behaviour in chapter 19 is classic extrovert, although I would want to challenge that, but look at what happens next. Elijah is threatened and he runs. Anyone might do that, especially given Jezebel's reputation, but he doesn't just flee; he disappears by himself. Verse 3 tells us that he leaves his servant and goes off into the desert alone. This sounds like an introvert withdrawing for security although it could describe a terrified extrovert; I repeat myself when I remind you that I am not arguing Elijah is one or the other, but rather that the behaviour he exhibits, and within which he meets God, is classically introvert.

He withdraws to be alone, and interacts with God under the broom tree, albeit sullenly and with a degree of nihilism. He then spends almost six weeks walking across the desert alone before reaching a cave. There he rests and encounters God, but that encounter is not in noise, or drama, or force… rather it is in the sound of silence.

Once again, and arguably this is a fairly normative pattern[2] until the coming of Christ, God's voice is heard in the place of solitude, withdrawal, and contemplation. The voice of God speaks in the inner place and is enacted in the outer world. The process of the prophet's engagement with God is primarily in language and methodology that is familiar to the introvert.

Jesus

Don't worry! I don't believe it is possible to prove that Jesus was an introvert (or an extrovert), but it is clear that He engages in patterns of behaviour which feed introverts, and provides a pattern of ministry to which an introvert can aspire without losing him- or her-self.

Thus Jesus often invests in deep and specific relationship, for example with Lazarus, Mary, and Martha as well as with the twelve. Moreover He is often found in specific conversation, even in apparently crowded situations (although it is not clear whether these conversations are the intimate one-to-one interactions one would expect of an introvert or the more boisterous group-chat of an extrovert). Notice, though, His interactions with Zacchaeus or Simon.[3]

Much of His teaching is done in intimate settings; I think of Nicodemus (John 3), for example, or the way he sends people out of the house before he heals Jairus' daughter (Mark 5:40). He clearly invests time and effort in the twelve and in a smaller group of Peter, James, and John. Jesus does introvert communication, and of course, His one-to-many communication also fits an introvert strength.

Moreover, Jesus clearly values time spent alone. Mark 1:35 sees Jesus getting up "very early in the morning while it is still dark" and going off alone to pray. Matthew and Luke have Him in the desert alone for forty days following His baptism. In Gethsemane we see Him withdrawing alone when under the greatest imaginable stress. Jesus practises the discipline of solitude and at key points we find Him by Himself.

With the coming of Christ we see God speaking in a social context in a new way, and this is arguably expanded further with the coming of the Spirit at Pentecost, but in Christ we still see that pattern of the individual seeking God in solitude and engaging alone in the disciplines of prayer and formation. Moreover, this healthy interaction with solitude and discipline does not end with Christ.

Paul

I often hear it argued that Paul was an extrovert, and possibly he was; however, he certainly didn't behave like one all the time. Look at the following passage from the first chapter of the epistle to the Galatians:

> I want you to know, brothers and sisters, that the gospel I preached is not of human origin. I did not receive it from any man, nor was I taught it; rather, I received it by revelation from Jesus Christ.
>
> For you have heard of my previous way of life in Judaism, how intensely I persecuted the church of God and tried to destroy it. I was advancing in Judaism beyond many of my own age among my people and was extremely zealous for the traditions of my fathers. But when God, who set me apart from my mother's womb and called me by his grace, was pleased to reveal his Son in me so that I might preach him among the Gentiles, my immediate response was not to consult any human being. I did not go up to Jerusalem to see those who were apostles before I was, but I went into Arabia. Later I returned to Damascus.
>
> Then after three years, I went up to Jerusalem to get acquainted with Cephas and stayed with him fifteen days. I saw none of the other apostles – only James, the Lord's brother. I assure you before God that what I am writing to you is no lie.
>
> (Galatians 1:11–20)

Here you have a public figure who is miraculously converted and is to be the apostle to the Gentile world. His own testimony is that the first three years of his discipleship are not in the energetic bosom of a growing church, and, let's face it, that's where most of us would want to have been, but rather in Arabia and Damascus. To be fair, we don't know what he did in those places or how his time was spent, but this withdrawal from the centre of activity is not typical of an extrovert, and in context the implication is that this time was spent in contemplation, consideration, and growth. It is from this time alone that the fruit of public ministry grew.

Mary and Martha

Consider the drama when Jesus arrives at Mary and Martha's house:

> As Jesus and his disciples were on their way, he came to a village where a woman named Martha opened her home to him. She had a sister called Mary, who sat at the Lord's feet listening to what he said. But Martha was distracted by all the preparations that had to be made. She came to him and asked, "Lord, don't you care that my sister has left me to do the work by myself? Tell her to help me!"
>
> "Martha, Martha," the Lord answered, "you are worried and upset about many things, but few things are needed – or indeed only one. Mary has chosen what is better, and it will not be taken away from her."
>
> (Luke 10:38–42)

Might it be possible that here we see the interaction of a classic introvert and a classic extrovert? If it is, which way round might they be?

Possibly we see Mary, the introvert, investing in the specific task of listening to Jesus and refusing to be distracted by the social whirl that might have inhabited the kitchen, with its many demands and high level of energy, while Martha enjoys her crowd but feels that she is missing out on action elsewhere.

Conversely, we might see Mary the extrovert joining the bustle around a charismatic teacher, while Martha works quietly away in the background, cherishing space but feeling increasingly "used".

Either (or neither) might be true, and Jesus' response speaks to all people alike, although the challenge is heard differently depending on who we are.

To misquote the writer to the Hebrews:

> what more shall I say? I do not have time to tell
> about Gideon, Barak, Samson and Jephthah,
> about David and Samuel and the prophets, who
> through faith [so often nurtured in the quiet place]
> conquered kingdoms, administered justice, and
> gained what was promised; who shut the mouths of
> lions, quenched the fury of the flames, and escaped
> the edge of the sword; whose weakness was turned
> to strength; and who became powerful in battle and
> routed foreign armies.
>
> (Hebrews 11:32–34, my words in brackets)

With my five examples and many others, we see that the Bible has space for introverts and draws all of us into some patterns of behaviour that come naturally to introverts. Conversely, it challenges those of us who are introvert to live beyond our comfort zones, just as it makes space for us to inhabit the deep calling that we observe within our created being. However, the Bible has far more to say to us about personality and character than simply giving us permission to explore engagement with God from within our type.

Some insights around personality from the Bible

The danger of a chapter like this in a book like this is that we miss the obvious in search of specifics. Introvert engagement with God is a crucial part of our relationship with Him, but there is much more to learn from the Bible than this. Once we have established that it is OK to be a Christian introvert we need to consider what type of introvert we should be. By this I do not mean that there is a template or a model introvert to which a faithful Christian should aspire, but rather that the image of God in which we have been created has been warped and stretched by our brokenness. Not everything that is within us is good, and if we are serious about the issues the Bible would raise we will find ourselves challenged as well as affirmed.

So here are a few insights, in vaguely canonical order: lessons that occur as we run our minds over the history of God's engagement with humanity as it has been passed to us.

The importance of relationship

One of the very first things that we see God saying about human beings is that it is not good for us to be alone. This is His rationale for creating woman, who brings opportunity for conversation, relationship, and family into the world. This is not to say that women are more extrovert than men or to ascribe introversion or extroversion to either Adam or Eve. It is, rather, to observe that the first need that God meets for humanity is addressing the emptiness of alone-ness.

Alone-ness in this sense is a very different kind of experience to solitude. Alone-ness veers towards isolation and loneliness, whereas solitude is a deliberate choice for space for a specific period of time. Both can be hard, but one is empty and the other is searching; one is enforced and the other is a gift; one is undermining and the other constructive.

One of the things that often surprises people as they engage with the question of introversion, particularly if they are not themselves introvert, is the observation that "introverts can be lonely too".[4] The introvert's need for space, and the essential task of "recharging batteries" in withdrawal, does not mean that isolation provides sufficient nourishment for the introvert. People need God and other people. This is part of healthy created order and it is rare that a call to holiness is a call to solitary life. This is why solitary isolation is such a profound punishment (even for introverts).

So it is that God creates community and institutes relationship at the heart of the created order. Indeed Genesis 1:26–27 indicates, through God referring to Himself in the plural and the image of God being revealed in our maleness and femaleness, that our "relationality" is part of that which is His image:

> Then God said, "Let us make mankind in our
> image, in our likeness, so that they may rule over
> the fish in the sea and the birds in the sky, over the
> livestock and all the wild animals, and over all the
> creatures that move along the ground."

So God created mankind in his own image, in
the image of God he created them; male and female
he created them.

Each of us is called to relationship; introvert or extrovert, we cannot be alone for all time. Other people matter.

The importance of solitude

That being said, solitude also matters. We have already thought about Elijah and his journey alone into the wilderness. We have seen Moses following a similar pattern. We could think about Abraham and his journey with Isaac to Mount Moriah. We see it in David's habit of withdrawing to desert places and I wonder if it is hinted at in the Psalms when the Psalmist refers to meditating in the night (when presumably he was alone or at least the only one awake).

There is also a tantalizing hint at the importance of solitude right at the beginning of the Scriptures. We tend not to notice the first half of Genesis 3:8 because we are so focused on what happens next; but why was God walking in the garden in the cool of the day? Certainly He intended to meet Adam and Eve; otherwise His calling for them in verse 9 is strange, but this does not present as a fixed rendezvous. One walks in a garden to find space, particularly "in the cool of the day". Do we see, perhaps, a picture of the Creator modelling "downtime", alone and taking a walk in a beautiful place and a comfortable environment?

The call to solitude becomes explicit in the New Testament. Matthew 6:6 famously tells of Jesus instructing us to pray alone behind closed doors. (Note that the Greek here is singular not plural, in marked contrast with most biblical teaching. See the next section for more exploration of this.) Here we see clearly that there is a value in solitude that goes beyond a pragmatic or fearful alone-ness, and which is of a very different order to the dreadful experience of loneliness which all of us know from time to time. This practice of withdrawal is deemed spiritually beneficial by the One who created us and calls us.

Again, the invitation of Christ will be heard differently by different people, but the call to a degree of solitude is a life-giving invitation to all, however it is received.

The role of community

Equally important in this scrapbook of insights into the calls that the Bible holds out before our developing personhood is the role of community. It is not sufficient to say that relationships matter, although they clearly do: community also matters. The entirety of the first five books of the Bible, for example, is explicitly devoted to the development of community. The people of Israel are given identity, land, rules for self-governance, values, and an inheritance. They are formed from the "family of a wandering Aramean"[5] into a great people.

The New Testament describes the introduction of the new covenant between God and humans. All too often this new relationship with God in Christ has been interpreted individualistically. The rediscovery of the necessity of personal conversion which is central to post-reformation Christianity all too frequently means we see our response to Christ solely as a personal activity. This is fundamentally out of step, though, with the New Testament itself. Think of the images that Paul uses to help us understand what it is to be Christian; almost all of them are plural or collective (for example, we are described as stones, parts of a plant, bits of a body, or members of an army) and even the metaphors that are singular usually describe an individual who is healthy as part of a bigger community (think of a child, soldier, or servant). Moreover, the words used for instruction in the New Testament are also normatively plural. Let me give you an example.

Think of 1 Peter 1:15–16: "But just as he who called you is holy, so be holy in all you do; for it is written: 'Be holy, because I am holy.'" We read this as an instruction to live holy lives. We interpret it as a call to repent of the things that we do which are detrimental to the image of God within us. We tend to think of this as a singular command. You, Jo Blogger, are to be a very holy person as you sit behind your desk this week. Don't steal work supplies, don't look at porn on your computer, do say some prayers, and do give to the poor. This is all helpful... but actually the words in Greek are plural. The call to holiness is primarily a communal one. We are called to be holy together, in the way we relate, in the way we communicate, in the way we respect, defend, pray for, worship with, and challenge each other. We are called to be in community and it is in such community that the life of the people of God is truly inhabited.

Solitude matters, but it is hard to argue for personhood in the Scriptures in anything other than community terms.

The call to stillness

I suppose that one of the first verses that comes to mind when we think about introversion in the Bible will be Psalm 46:10, "Be still and know that I am God", which is ironic given that it has little to do with personal stillness when read in context (it is about God stilling wars and bringing peace in order that His glory might be re-established). Such exegetical niceties are often overlooked in the Psalms as "deep calls to deep" (for example, Psalm 42:7, which is more explicitly concerned with water than the soul) because they speak of truths that we know we need to hear.

This is how it is with the call to stillness. There is a repeated call to pause and consider. We see it in the meditation encouraged in the Psalms. We see it in the methods used by prophets such as Micaiah (1 Kings 22) or Jeremiah who clearly call on kings and people to pause and listen. Stillness matters, and, hard though it is to achieve, this is a deep call on the healthy soul.

The pursuit of wisdom

Wisdom is a treasure beyond value, and a gift that cannot be priced. It is, however, the great overlooked spiritual gift: misunderstood, undervalued, overlooked, and tragically unsought. When was the last time you heard it preached about, praised, or prayed for? Yet when the young Solomon was offered anything he wanted by God, this is what he sought, and "the Lord was pleased" that this was what he had requested (1 Kings 3:10).

The Bible as a whole presents this wisdom as the core calling of those who seek to follow faithfully. We are repeatedly told that the "fear of the Lord is the beginning of wisdom" (see Proverbs 1:7, 9:10; Psalm 19:9, 111:10, for example). This is a key phrase because no one can be in any doubt that the fear of the Lord is a fundamental calling for all who would worship God: fear, that is, in the sense of awe, wonder, worship, and respect; fear that is expressed as "faith" in the New Testament. If this "fear" or "faith" is just the beginning of wisdom, and all are called to such a beginning, is the invitation not implicit?

Indeed the invitation becomes explicit in the heart of the Old Testament, in what we often call the "wisdom literature". Here, for example, in the first nine chapters of the book of

Proverbs, wisdom is presented as an almost divine person, the lady Sophia. She invites the faithful to follow and not be distracted; to seek and inhabit wisdom. The invitation is one of desire, health, and reward, and has a highly relational dynamic to it. And this is not confined to the Old Testament. James, for example, instructs us to ask God for wisdom. Interestingly, John begins his great prologue by presenting Christ as the Logos, the word of God... echoing the wisdom of God.

This gift of wisdom, which leads to life and subverts our warped and injurious power structures, is not found in wealth, position, or gender. In particular, it is not to be found among "the foolish" who are loud, confident, hedonistic, and ultimately doomed. It is hidden and to be sought. Job famously searches creation for it (Job 28), and only finds it with God. It is a deep and profound calling on and for all of us who are created in the image of God who is the source and essence of all wisdom.

Where, then, is wisdom to be explored?

> One who spares words is knowledgeable; one who
> is cool in spirit has understanding.
> Even fools who keep silent are considered wise;
> when they close their lips, they are deemed
> intelligent.
>
> (Proverbs 17:27–28, NRSV)

> Who is wise and understanding among you? By
> his good conduct let him show his works in the
> meekness of wisdom.
>
> (James 3:13, ESV)

> But when you pray, go into your room, close the
> door and pray to your Father, who is unseen. Then

> your Father, who sees what is done in secret, will
> reward you. And when you pray, do not keep on
> babbling like pagans, for they think they will be
> heard because of their many words. Do not be like
> them...
>
> (Matthew 6:6–8, NIVUK)

The implication is clear: wisdom is found in a deep and persistent search for, and contemplation of, God. This is not the exclusive preserve of the introvert, of course, but wisdom is explored more fully in contemplation than celebration. It is relished with few words.

Jesus taught that our heart would be where our treasure was (Matthew 6:21). At first glance it looks as if He was talking of money, but His words are more broadly applicable than to mere materialism: in particular, they are true socially too. If we devote our time solely to the company of others, hanging on their words and whims, and longing more than anything to please them, we should not be surprised when what our lives produce is social acceptability rather than the "fruit" or "gifts" of the Spirit.

The commission to love, to pray, and to go

Finally, we do need to reflect that the Scriptures as a whole do not call us to self-service. One of the first recorded fruits of the fall is the murder of one brother by the other. When questioned by God Cain protests that he "is not his brother's keeper". The clear implication, which we see echoed throughout the Bible, is that this is not a sufficient response: he is not his brother's keeper, but he is his brother's brother. The elder brother does have cause to grieve over the prodigal. The hunter and the herdsman do belong together. We are called to be responsible for each other. This communality is at the heart of the Old Testament Law, the message of the prophets, and the concept and subsequent condemnation of Israelite kingship.

As Christians we are called beyond ourselves in numerous ways. We are instructed to love by our Lord (John 13:34). This is not an optional extra and the love in question is not a theoretical command confined to the emotions. It is hands-on, practical, committed stuff. We are instructed to pray – to do so faithfully, simply, continuously, and in an informed manner.

Jesus' parting words, according to Matthew, were to send us out to the very ends of the earth. Few of us are called to a hermitage; we are sent out. More particularly, we are sent to people with a message of grace, forgiveness, and life.

For some this is easy. For others it is really hard. It is, however, part of who we are called to be, whether this is a joy or part of the cross that we daily take up.

The God who "knit you together in your mother's womb" knows you and loves you (see Psalm 139:13). It doesn't matter whether you are male, female, young, old, black, white, introvert, or extrovert; He invites you to be shaped by Him daily. The remarkable thing is that, as your Creator shapes you, you find you are more yourself than you have ever been.

A Letter to Charismatics from an Introvert Among You

My dear charismatic brothers and sisters,

This is a letter many years in the making written by one who is glad to be one of you but who often feels alone in your company; one who delights in your fellowship, who finds himself freed by your generous joy and optimistic faith, and yet walks at times with a limp brought on by wrestling to conform to things that are desirable but don't quite come naturally. It is a warm letter, made possible by your loving encouragement and gracious acceptance, written with a smile as I seek to capture the banter and fun that we have enjoyed as we have explored our minor differences held together in the vast common heritage we have in Christ. We are created together in the image of the One.

What we share and celebrate together is profound, holy, and enriching both for us as disciples and for the world that we seek to serve. When I am with my charismatic family, my faith is lifted, my heart is encouraged, my feeble will is strengthened, and I am drawn into the things of the kingdom, not least through your fairly constant encouragement and the characteristic charismatic refusal to recognize an empty glass.

I must confess, though, that I wonder if we might not benefit from giving our vocal chords some "downtime"?

I know that not all charismatics are extrovert – indeed I am living proof of this – but our shared culture is very outgoing and silence, even quiet, appears to be unsettling. I am never sure why a people who profess attentiveness to the God who sometimes chooses to appear in the "sound of silence" **(I am thinking of 1 Kings 19 here)** rather than the earthquake, wind or fire, would make so little time to attend to the quieter harmonics of His grace and power.

While I think of it, can I observe that volume is not a good indicator of reliability? It is possible to be quiet and unwise, just as it is common to be loud and wrong. Today, though, this obvious truth often seems obscured: the more certain we are, the more excited and voluble we become, and thus when someone is passionate we assume they are right. They might be, but the eloquent enthusiast will be in error more often than they sound like they are! Volume shouldn't ever short-circuit reflection or erode wisdom.

Conversely, though, when we meet a quiet person who has the knack of making themselves heard we find ourselves so wrong-footed by their countercultural calm that we assume they are offering wisdom. Quiet authority appears to imply the possession of knowledge or insight, and sometimes this is right, but none can search for wisdom unless they quieten themself and give serious attention to the One who is always beyond and yet always near.

True listening gives careful attention to what is really being said and this always takes effort, whatever our personality. I sometimes jest by saying that extroverts need to work as hard at listening to the words introverts say as we do at not listening to every word *they say. All of us need to work at it and encourage the other in being truly heard, and it is about attending to another: whether we are thinking out loud or silently, the more we focus on what we want to say the harder it is to hear another, whether human or divine.*

It might appear as if introverts "hold all the aces here" because we are naturally quieter, but actually this only means the chatter is going on inside our heads. Extroverts do have some advantages when it comes to stilling themselves. We who are fluent in the inner place might appear quiet, but in honesty we all need encouragement in this discipline of stillness.

Moreover, those of us who naturally value the treasure of the silent place of listening struggle particularly when another's self-expression is constantly forced upon us so that we have to deal with our own chatter and theirs. It is so vital that we learn to pause for long enough to give attention – attention to God and to self, and genuine attention to the other.

Attention, you see, is far better given than sought. The gift of attention builds up; the seeking after attention puffs up. The gift brings security, the seeking only the desire for more. The gift builds relationship and embodies love; the seeking pushes all but the sycophant away. The gift progresses conversation and fruitful cooperation; the seeking only serves to pause proceedings while ego is satisfied. Most importantly, attention can be given to another while the eyes of our hearts are firmly focused on Jesus, but when we begin to seek attention our gaze is drawn to the thing to which our heart is giving its devotion, be that self or someone or something else.

Our calling, of course, is to be those whose attention is utterly fixed on Christ. We are to be as single-minded as a dog quivering with anticipation, whose eyes will not leave its master. We are to be as rapt as the teenager whose heartthrob has just entered the room. We are to give our devotion only to One – we worship one God – and while there are many ways to do the worshipping it is vital to allow space for each to move beyond the mechanics into the worship, beyond conformity and into encounter. And in this regard I do need to ask you a favour...

... please would you stop telling me what to do when we are worshipping? It might give you immense pleasure to see me joining the crowd in jumping, shouting, hugging, swaying, or generally jiggling for Jesus, but in order to do so I need to drag my attention away from Him, focus on you, and struggle to get over my embarrassment at doing a silly thing in order to fit in with the crowd. Surprisingly, one of the blessings of charismatic worship for introverts is that we can be anonymous in a crowd whose focus is the same as ours: no one is looking at me so I can simply concentrate on Jesus. That concentration is broken when someone gets the bright idea that a Mexican wave would somehow enhance the glory of God.

By the way, introverts are OK when we are quiet; this is part of our normal state of being. Please don't assume we are offended, offhand, disagreeing, or disinterested and do believe us when we say we are fine. It is lovely to have people ask the concerned question, but somewhat irritating to be pestered just for inhabiting our natural state.

The truth is that we want to be with you; otherwise we wouldn't be there! Although that reminds me to say that time feels quite different to an introvert. Interacting with others uses up our energy rather than energizing us. This means that many of us will subconsciously know when a meeting will finish and it will feel like we have used up all of our energy by that point. It's as if we ration our fuel and we are empty by the end of the meeting. When meetings run over time, we have no more resources to draw upon and struggle not to be tired or grumpy. Being "hijacked" straight after a meeting is particularly hard, which is partly why the toilets are a popular destination at the end of a long gathering! Even a few minutes to recharge the battery in a place where it is permissible to be alone makes a massive difference.

So much of this is about little things, like this, which make a big difference. Charismatics are pragmatic by inclination, though, so we can deal with this. This pragmatism, which arises from our tendency to ask if we can see God at work in something, is one of the things that is most apparent to the reflective among us. Charismatics tend to get things done and make things work, and this is great, but over-pragmatism does have a downside. Pragmatism unsupported by common sense and careful discipline does not lead to long-term health. So, for example, if we, as a movement, are not reflective or careful about our theology we will go the way of other enthusiastic movements before us. We might grow churches in the short-term, but we also need to look to long-term health. We need to be alert, when our appreciation of a great speaker lessens our desire to ask the difficult questions about holiness, orthodoxy, or consistency. Or when our desire to "be at the cutting edge of what God is doing" overrides the tough challenge that clearly mattered to Jesus as He prayed in John 17. Doing the "stuff that works" is really important, but let's not let it allow us to be short-sighted or foolish, however attractive the fruits of myopia and folly might appear. Perhaps the irritating introvert has a role in remembering this which is as vital as our being stretched beyond our naturally reserved comfort zone.

Now, please hear me; I am not accusing charismatics or extroverts of foolishness, lack of wisdom, or other inferiorities, although I do fear that I may be heard in that way. I observe, both in myself and others, that deep insecurities often come out when we talk about personality and spirituality. Introverts feel that they are not as good as extroverts because we can't keep going in public all day, and extroverts feel that they are not as holy, spiritual, wise or prayerful as they could, or maybe should, be. Noticing this insecurity matters, not least because when an extrovert feels insecure they appear to feel the need to make others behave like them to bolster their own identity. This urge, combined with spiritual hunger and fervour and an external culture, can at times be tricky to negotiate unscathed.

Our security, our identity, our joy, and our unity is in Christ and in Him alone.

None of this means that introverts are better than anyone else. We need each other and I am deeply grateful for the ways you reach out to me and allow me to reach out to you. I notice, though, that this is in conflict with the insecurity that lies, acknowledged or not, at the heart of fallen people like us. It's so easy, as we reflect on difference, only to see the things that others do better than us, particularly for those of us who hang around in charismatic circles, because we don't really have a body-theology. We talk "body of Christ" talk, but our dependence on the Spirit's provision often leads us to expect that we have all the gifts that we need all of the time (instead of seeing the truth that we will have the gifts we need when we need them, whether they are given through us or another. This is the kind of God we serve). When put so starkly this is obviously dangerous: no one person is perfect or has every gift, but instead of living in the freedom of our interdependence we allow ourselves to be blind to this simple truth and live with a feeling of nonspecific guilt that we are not good at something precious. When God gives me a gift He might do so directly, or He might do so through you. Both are good and special.

Our kingdom theology, so rightly focused on the present and coming rule and reign of Christ is, too often, insubstantial and insufficient when it comes to a full inhabiting of the body of Christ. Recall what Paul writes in 1 Corinthians: we, as human beings called into the body of Christ, have been created as a part of a bigger whole rather than just a stand-alone unit. When we truly live together as part of the church, the bride of Christ, our very existence honours our Lord and exhibits worship at the most fundamental level.

Obviously this teaching needs careful handling; just because prayer does not come naturally to you does not mean that you don't need to pray. However, it does mean that we pray as we can and allow ourselves to be enriched, supported, encouraged, and nurtured by those for whom prayer comes instinctively. More than *that, because we are the body of Christ we are called to commit ourselves to releasing and encouraging those who bring complementary gifts to our own.*

What I am trying to say is that I am glad that you are you, and what I am saying should not be taken to imply that I would like you to be different. I need you, and want you to be more fully you.

So... *thank you. Thank you for your humour and your enthusiasm. Thank you for your patience and your faith. Thank you for keeping going and keeping me going. Thank you for making it so clear that I matter to you. Thank you for not being perfect and not expecting me to be either.*

With my gratitude and ongoing prayers,

Your introvert brother

4

What Do We Mean by "Charismatic"?

Up to this point we have been talking almost exclusively about introversion and our rich but noisy modern Western context. This book, though, is entitled *The Introvert Charismatic*, and both words matter. The phrase captures something which at first is surprising, but then appears to make profound sense about the idea of "introversion" and "charismatic-ness" being in the same sentence.

Recall something I quoted earlier (see page 33): "The phrase 'introverted charismatic' is interesting. The negative associations I have with both words are significantly mitigated when they are put together. 'Introverted' softens my stereotype of noisy arm-waving loons. 'Charismatic' softens my stereotype of nerdy awkwardness. Put together the words suggest a person of gentleness, stillness, strength, depth, openness to God's Spirit, a person who is quietly observant, notices what God is about – there are connotations of wisdom here."

We do need to do some careful work, though, on what we mean by "charismatic", because it is a term which often appears loaded but which is loaded in different ways depending on where and who you are. An early draft of this book was written while on retreat in Canada, having just spent a few days in the States. There the terms "charismatic" and "renewal" carry with them a particular meaning in a manner they don't in the UK. However, all terms have undertones and it's helpful to clarify what I am and what I am not meaning.

I am writing as someone rooted in the British church. Compared with North America we regard "charismatic" as more of a general term indicating an emphasis on the kingdom, an openness to the tangible but still numinous presence of the Spirit of God, and an expectation that God can be seen to answer prayer. It is a word describing enthusiasts, and has overtones of activism, but it is not one for which there would be a universal, agreed definition.

One of the lectures I give each year at college is on "charismatic spirituality", and for that I have surveyed leaders for their understanding of "charismatic". These are some of the definitions that I have been given.

"I would define a charismatic as…

… a person consciously reliant on the Holy Spirit to work within and through them."

… one who is actively open to the presence of the Spirit in the everyday, open to words, pictures, tongues, the exercise of healing ministry. A charismatic is one who seeks the Spirit, who is expectant that God meets us in worship and lifts us up, though that worship could be very traditional.

Has the term 'charismatic' been overly associated with a style of worship, rather than a theological understanding of the work of the Spirit?"

… someone who is filled with and dependent on the Spirit of Jesus, seeking to exercise gifts of the Spirit and express the fruit of the Spirit."

… those who live within the understanding of God's gifts to us. The term has been pushed too much, in my mind, to the specific list of spiritual gifts given in Paul's writings but I feel that that is too restrictive to a God who is abundant in his giving… I am a charismatic because I believe strongly in God's unending blessing to his children to equip them for the tasks he calls them to. I believe God calls us today as he did thousands of years ago and he can equip us with the gifts we need to fulfil them. The gifts he gives to us should be used for those tasks and we should return to him daily, even moment by moment, to receive again new gifts and fresh calling.

I believe God's gifts are supernatural in that they are more natural than we imagine."

"I hate labels – because 'charismatic' simply means moving in the Spirit… so I am sure all Christians would sign up for that. But I suppose the label goes with those who love to recognize, emphasize, and revel in the outpouring of the Spirit in every aspect of life (the up, in, and out) so, as I love to

revel in the works of the Spirit, I'm happy to wear
the badge."

By "charismatic" all I mean is a person or a people who believe
in and look for the active "charisms" – *charis* (χάρις) is a Greek
word used frequently in the New Testament which means
"grace" – that is, the graces, marks, gifts, or characteristics of
the Spirit of God. We do have an extraordinary propensity
for getting our theological knickers into an ecclesiastical twist
about things "charismatic", but it is not really complicated. In
fact simplicity is almost a doctrine for me; Jesus said we were
to be like children, one of the implications of which is that if
something doesn't have a simplicity at heart then we probably
haven't really understood it yet.

I would argue that being a Christian who is in step with
a biblical understanding of following Christ requires that we
engage with the charisms of God, and thus with the charisms of
the Spirit of God. There is a simple framework for this, which
would include the following uncontentious and theologically
orthodox tenets:

God created the world, the universe, and all that is in them,
all that has been and all that will be. This creating act arises
from and establishes His Lordship over all, His commitment to
all, and His knowledge of all.[1]

Our choice as humans was, and continues to be, that of
rebellion. We can argue about details but at our core we incline
towards self-determination rather than true worship and this
represents fundamental discontinuity within the created order.
We choose the sovereignty of self and thus find ourselves
disconnected from the kingship and kingdom of God. This
shatters the implicit covenant of creation and leads to separation
and death which pollutes the entire created order.[2]

God, in the person of Jesus, broke into this estranged world with the aim and intention of revelation, rescue, and re-creation. His arrival, actions, and teaching heralded the coming "kingdom of God". He taught the new covenant of love, and His death and resurrection opened the way for those who "receive Him and call upon Him" to enter the promise.[3]

He taught His disciples to pray that the kingdom would come and God's will would be done, to wait for the coming of the Spirit, to make disciples of all the earth, and to expect His imminent return.[4]

We live in that in-between time, when the gift of salvation and the outpouring of the Spirit of God have been established, but Christ is yet to return and bring in the new creation, the fullness of the kingdom of God. In this time we are called and commissioned to inhabit the coming work of God and proclaim the good news that "the kingdom of God is at hand", inviting people to repent, reimagine, relearn, and believe the good news! (Mark 1:15, RSV). We are heralds, ambassadors, messengers, servants, or children of that kingdom. We proclaim it; we live it; we trust it; we pray for it; we work for it; we long for it.

Forgive me if this all looks a bit obvious; that is almost the point. This is the gospel that we believe; being charismatic is not really remarkable. Two more clarifications might be in order, though.

Firstly, what do I mean by "the kingdom of God"? The kingdom of God is simply where God is King. That means that it is a place where His will and His way hold sway, for it is a place where His reign is fully established. It is a dominion within which we find life, forgiveness, salvation, healing, wholeness, love, grace, and so on because this is the nature and person of the King.

Secondly, if we are called to be heralds or ambassadors of

the kingdom, which is how Paul describes himself in Ephesians 6:20, what will that look like? Ambassadors bear the nature of the King to those to whom they are sent. In no particular order:

They wear the regalia of the kingdom – they bear the likeness of their King.

They are distinctive in their speech and outlook.

They do the works of the King.

They are clear where they belong.

They carry the authority of the King.

Such is the calling, to one degree or another, of any ambassador. They provide a neat description of what I mean by "charismatic". All of these marks are brought to birth within us in and through the ministry of the Spirit. Let me unpack this a little.

They wear the regalia of the kingdom

Jesus instructed His disciples to wait in Jerusalem until they "had been clothed with power from on high" (Luke 24:49). They were not to do anything, despite the fact that He had died for them and been raised from the dead, until God had clothed them in the regalia of the kingdom. This clothing was not mere finery like the scarlet of a Beefeater; neither was it simple functionality like a soldier's Combat 95s; here is the nature of God Himself being poured out on His children. So Paul, in his letter to the Christians in Colossae, urges them to clothe themselves with compassion, kindness, and humility, and other characteristic virtues of the King, and over them all to put on love, the very nature of God (3:12–14). Elsewhere he instructs the Ephesians to put on the armour of God (6:10–18), and again this is not the functional gadgets of Christian living, but truth, righteousness, the Spirit of God Himself. We who have been baptized in Christ are clothed in Christ (Galatians 3:27).

A charismatic, in the sense I am using the term, is one who is clothed with power in the person of the God Himself, most usually experienced in the person of the Holy Spirit. The truth of this is profound: see an ambassador and you see the King; touch a Christian, and in a profound sense you are in contact with the Spirit of God. We are not God-like in our nature: we remain weak and foolish in our humanity, but we are clothed. We are fallible but held. We wear the regalia of the kingdom.

This is the calling of the charismatic, and it is a high calling indeed. It is why holiness and discipline are central, although too often absent, dynamics of charismatic discipleship.

They are distinctive in their speech and outlook

Ambassadors are known by their speech. They will be both fluent in the language of the kingdom and able to speak to the people to whom they are sent. They carry a message from the King and they deliver it faithfully and consistently. That message might be a specific instruction or it might be the enactment of a policy, but the faithful herald will be true to it. This is one reason the comedy of Jonah with its simple but demanding challenge to deliver a message from God is so central to the Bible.

So it is with Christians, specifically for charismatic Christians. Our conversation should be that of heaven, although we are fluent in the language of the world. It is significant that three of the earliest gifts post-Pentecost are that of glossolalia, or tongues (Acts 2:4), of preaching (Acts 2:14ff), and that of words of supernatural knowing (Acts 5:1–10) or wisdom (Acts 6:10), both of which evidence the prophetic gifting of the followers of Christ. Here are gifts of speech; the gift of speaking in a prayer language to and with the Father, of speaking out the Father's word in proclamation, and of giving specific instruction from God. We speak the language of the kingdom and, while that is true for all Christians, those who are charismatic would expect to engage in this in ways which go beyond the "normal" or "rational" as they engage with the speaking God who speaks through His children.

More than that, though, even when humans are speaking "normally" we speak with an accent. Visit the US with a British accent and person after person will observe that you are "not from around here." We are recognized in part by our speech. So it is for the Christian. Our citizenship is in a different kingdom, our conversation is different, and this will be seen and heard in us and through us. So it comes as no surprise that our conversation is to be "seasoned with salt" (Colossians 4:6), and that we are to allow our minds to dwell on that which we have been taught and that which is good, pure, lovely, and admirable (Philippians 4:8–9).

Again this is partly descriptive, and partly a challenge for the modern charismatic. We should be distinctive in our speech, not just because we are informal and cheerful. Our conversation, whether or not we are "speaking a word from God" should reflect the speech of heaven. This is a high calling which will shape what we watch and read, and where we give our attention.

They do the works of the King

Ambassadors must walk the walk as well as talking the talk and looking the part. A true ambassador is not simply a messenger, although they will be willing to be, and at times they might wish they were. We live as representative citizens of the kingdom wherever we are.

So it is that those who follow Christ in the Scriptures (in both the Old and New Testaments) are marked out by the most remarkable things happening. People are healed around them (as in 2 Kings 5 or Acts 5, for example), the dead are raised (as in 1 Kings 17 and Acts 20), and, most significantly, others find their way into the kingdom through the works of those who proclaim.

Charismatics are those who take Jesus' instruction on seeing the works of the kingdom seriously and get on and make space for them. They pray for healing, they oppose the demonic, and they expect to see the gifts that Paul spells out in 1 Corinthians 12 and 14 lived out in action. The works of the kingdom, in other words, are not just works that the King does in a distant place. For here is the mystery of being a herald. Jesus sends us to the places He is about to go just as he did with the twelve and the seventy (see Luke 9 and 10). We don't go off on our own. We are commissioned to announce Him and then do what He is doing. Matthew 28 is clear: He has all authority and therefore we must go because He is with us in our very act of going.

Unfortunately this engagement in works of power can seem to divide us rather than unite us. There are often schools of practice that evolve around particular styles or individuals and this is to our shame. We are different, but we have a common call to do as Jesus did and this goes beyond any of us. My notes scribbled on a first draft of this chapter have at this point, "End of Mark???", which I jotted down to remind myself to consider referring readers to the disputed text at the end of Mark's Gospel as more evidence of what the early church, at the very least, thought would mark us out. I had to smile when I came back to that note, though: in truth, all of this "ministry" is beyond me. I cannot do it, and when I try to I end up distorting it and damaging those I am trying to help. It is usually when "Mark" (me) ends and Jesus starts that I can truly engage in this dynamic of discipleship which is entirely grace (*charis*).

This is the distinction that the Canadian Vineyard leader and teacher Gary Best helpfully draws between "ambassador" and "general". Both have real authority, but only the general has might. When the general is disobeyed he has to sort it out; when the ambassador is frustrated it is the King who is in control. Our authority is not actually our authority; it is the coming King in whose name we operate and we must never forget this.

They are clear where they belong

If an ambassador is to remain a good ambassador they will never forget that they are a citizen of their own land, subjects of their sovereign. They will respect the local authority and even mostly live under its laws and regulations, but they belong elsewhere. So it is with charismatics: our eyes are fixed, not on the problems of the situation in which we find ourselves or the politics of our current position, but on the nature and activity of the One who commissions us. We have seen the glory of the King and our lives are dedicated to bringing the glorious liberty of his Fatherhood to those around us. We are citizens, not of earth, but of heaven (Philippians 3:20).

This is what Jesus – our teacher, inspiration, Saviour, and

Lord – did and it is what He taught us to do (John 5:19). Thus we are unrepentant and unashamed about our passion and our conviction: we are committed to a different agenda despite the cost it might incur. We are people of the kingdom of God and long for as many as possible to hear the life-giving invitation of our King to join Him.

This is another challenge from and to the charismatic world. If we believe this then we do need to work seriously hard on how we develop and maintain our citizenship. We can often feel that we are living a long way from home. The charismatic world is not one in which patient discipline is highly prized, as our rather pragmatic and experiential practice can draw us to value immediacy over sustainability and froth over fruit. Discipline and commitment, however, are exactly what aliens and strangers need if they are not merely to assimilate.

They carry the authority of the King

Finally, a good herald will carry authority because they know something of the mind of the King. We do need to be careful here, as I began to explore above, because teaching in this area seems to me to fall into one of two equal and opposite errors.

Sometimes we can give the impression that the herald is the king, but the great danger in this is immediately apparent. We are given authority, but this is delegated not absolute authority. We are sent off not as warrior lords with a mini-kingdom to dominate or even as generals with a battle to command, but rather as sons and daughters. We are part of the family, and we join in with the Father's words and works. Thus Jesus did what He saw the Father doing (John 5:19), and we are called to be those who participate in the work of God.

Ministry is about making space and seeing what God does and then blessing it, rather than deciding what He will do and commanding it. John Wimber, the remarkable Californian pastor and teacher who brought this fresh teaching about the ministry of the Holy Spirit to so much of the church in the West, was once in Poland at a very large and remarkable gathering of Polish leaders. He taught and then made some space for the Spirit to come. Often, even usually, when he did this remarkable things would happen; indeed, that was what he was known for. On this occasion, though, nothing happened. John suggested that it was, therefore, time for coffee. Apparently the organizers came up to him and said that they couldn't break before God had done something significant. John replied that he couldn't do anything God was not doing, and if He wasn't going to do stuff then "coffee's good"!

Our authority doesn't mean that "our will should be done", but neither does it mean that we are irrelevant. This is the other error into which we so easily fall. When God created He gave dominion to humanity (Genesis 1:28–30). He has not altered His promise, and that is, at least in part, why redemption could only come in and through a human being – Jesus the new Adam. God rarely, if ever, acts in this world apart from through human agency. We are His children, and He takes great joy in working with us and through us. Thus we are called on to take authority and exercise it alongside Him. It is not for our ends or purpose; it is not for our glory or fame. It is by Him, for Him, and with Him, but we need to participate. This is why Jesus gave his followers authority, whether it was to forgive sins (John 20:23), to heal, to drive out demons (see Luke 9:1), or to make disciples (see Matthew 28:19). We carry the authority of the King, and it takes careful but bold determination to do so appropriately.

What, then, do I mean by a charismatic? I mean someone who walks in the fullness of the Spirit of God; someone who seeks to do the work that Jesus commissioned in the power of the Spirit and to the glory of the Father. I mean a Christian who is committed to the kingdom of God in all its fullness; someone who has repented and believes the good news, who longs for the coming of the King and rejoices over every small sign of that coming and glorious presence.

I don't necessarily mean someone who is weird, or forceful, or loud (although they could be any or all of those). I don't mean someone from one particular camp or "school". I just mean a really ordinary, biblical, growing, and learning Christian in all the full wonder of that name, open to the remarkable tangible presence of God in and through His Holy Spirit.

Meet Bob

Bob (whose name has been changed) writes, "I have been a Christian for most of my life. I have been in some form of Christian leadership since my mid-teens and in paid leadership positions for almost twenty years. I am a deeply rooted, but gentle, evangelical and for most of that time I have been around the things that others would describe as charismatic, a title of which I am a little cautious. I tend towards talking of renewal or 'the things of the Spirit', although I recognize that neither of these terms is without its problems. As time has gone on I have taken on different leadership positions in things of an evangelical and charismatic persuasion.

"However, I have always wondered, secretly, whether I really was 'charismatic'. I am naturally quiet and I prefer to look and see what God is doing and then join in, as opposed to having 'faith' that I can make a particular thing take place. I am cautious of personal charisma taking the place of the leadership which God wants to offer through His Spirit and yet I live in a world where strong and dramatic leadership is often revered. As a result I have to confess that I have often tried to step into the role of a charismatic leader. This has not been without 'success', and critical self-reflection would conclude that my motives have usually been more good than bad, but... it has never really been me, and those who know me see clearly when I am trying too hard. More than that, I have found it a very unhealthy way to live spiritually.

"It is so easy to think that I need to do the same things as everyone else if I want to 'step into' the things of God. Because He is always beyond me I do get easily confused as to what is Him at work and what is people's response to Him. This is especially true when people are really overwhelmed by His goodness and we think that the reaction that they have is actually the action of God. Actually, just as it takes two to tango, so the presence of God will be manifested differently in every single person, because we are not merely empty vessels. God invites us to dance with Him and each of us will do that differently. I know this... but it is still hard to live in the freedom it should bring.

"Some years ago I had the privilege of hosting a teacher by the name of Gary Best who heads up the Vineyard Churches in Canada. He came to do a New Wine 'Kingdom Day' at the church I was then leading, and to be honest I was blown away. Here was an international speaker and leader who turned up at my house the night before the event and went straight off to his room to rest. Where were the lengthy stories of his own success, which I realize now I had been dreading (they always make me feel a failure), but which I had been expecting as this visiting leader sought to encourage me?

"The next day was no less shocking: Gary sat on one of my kitchen stools at the front of church and chatted quietly with the 200 people who had gathered. Here was someone whose ministry consisted of waiting and seeing what God was up to and then blessing it. Here

was a man who was clearly an introvert and God was (and is) using him mightily.

"It was as if God was slapping me round the face with a wet fish and telling me to wake up. He didn't make a mistake when He made me. He loves me as I am and that's how He wants to use me. The next morning in church, as if to make a point, I saw the most significant healing I have ever seen. The Spirit of God is not interested in our personality type. All (s)he wants is those who will be obedient and let Her work. We are called to participate in the work of the kingdom and all people can do that if they will hear and obey.

"I don't think I have this taped, by any means, but I am exploring what it means to be me and to be fully inhabiting 'the glorious liberty of the children of God'. There are many bits of me that still need to be redeemed and made holy, so I can't just say that I am who I am, because I am a work in progress. However, my being an introvert is not sinful or broken; it is part of the gift of who I am and when offered as a living sacrifice is a profound part of the life of worship to which I am called. This is how I am seeking to live."

5

Charismatics Throughout History

W ikipedia dates the start of the charismatic movement to 1960 and the start of Pentecostalism to the early 1900s. In a technical sense this is not unfair, but it is rather too narrow for our purposes and gives the unhelpful idea that engagement with things charismatic is novel or recent in origin.

I realize that this is one of the key points where you could choose to disagree with me and throw out the bathwater, but I am arguing that there is no one coherent definition of the word "charismatic" which permits us to use it in a pseudo-denominational sense. "Charismatic" is a word like "spirituality" or even "sexuality", which we use to describe something we know in general and find hard to pin down specifically or precisely. For the evangelical world this looser use of language is both good and bad. It represents a healthy intellectual and spiritual humility which is beginning to embrace mystery in a life-giving manner. It is concerning, though, that there appears to be a broad trend among evangelicals towards reification and generalization which leads us away from some of the tougher and more disciplined parts of our distinctive calling.

There are characteristics that unite charismatics, but they are fewer than we might at first think and often make the word more helpful as an adjective than a noun, contrary to my usage in the titles of this book and this chapter. Charismatics will be explicitly reliant on the work of the Holy Spirit and expectant that God will be responsive and tangibly active in the world around. They will tend towards some kind of "kingdom theology", although there will not be unanimity when it comes to defining what that means. There is a strong tendency towards theological orthodoxy (which is a word meaning "right believing" – that what we believe is in line with what most Christians have believed through the ages. These beliefs are concisely expressed in the creeds).[1]

Charismatics are a varied bunch. You will find charismatic Catholics and charismatic liberals and charismatics who think they are one thing but may well be something else![2] There are charismatic evangelicals of all shades of evangelicalism. There are a great many charismatics who seem to confound any neat "boxing", and one is often surprised by particular views individuals hold. This is important because the question of how people define and protect orthodoxy is a really useful tool to review the heart of a movement.

I was brought up as an evangelical (and you will have picked up that this is still my heartland) and as such I was taught that the test of orthodoxy was whether something was "biblical". As an alert young Christian I quickly picked up that "biblical" meant a particular interpretation of the Bible so that, for example, women did not have to cover their heads or be silent, though it would have pleased me to tell my little sister to be quiet and learn in due submission from my father and me (see

1 Timothy 2:11–12)! For those of a more traditional catholic persuasion orthodoxy is preserved in the teaching of the church. It is becoming increasingly common today for orthodoxy (or "believing right") merely to be practically defined in some kind of loving orthopraxy (or "doing right"), but this might be a red herring for our current enquiry. The question is what is the mark of orthodoxy for those who are charismatic?

Observation suggests that the most obvious mark of orthodoxy for the charismatic is the tangible presence of the Holy Spirit. This is usually held in creative tension with other marks of orthodoxy, but if "God is clearly active" then someone will be given an attentive hearing. Obviously this comes with the health warning that we must be wary of charlatans and fraudsters who merely appear to be acting out of some kind of anointing, and I wonder if this caution lies behind the relational nature of many charismatic leadership structures. We learn to look for fruit grown through long-term faithfulness that is in keeping with the kingdom being proclaimed. Such a mark of orthodoxy, while clearly open to abuse, should not be too quickly dismissed. It has similarities, at the very least, to what we see the disciples looking for in the book of Acts. Think of Peter and Cornelius in Acts 10: Peter is persuaded that the Gentiles can be baptized because they are speaking in tongues and praising God and have thus clearly had the Holy Spirit "poured out" upon them.

This is why I want to use the term as a general rather than a specific descriptor of those who are expectant and longing that the Spirit of God will be active among us here and now in this in-between time establishing the rule and reign of God among us in both natural and supernatural ways. This kind of Christianity has not been invented in the last fifty years; it goes all the way back to Christ, and the bulk of the rest of this chapter is a quick series of snapshots of some of the highlights of that journey. We have already noted something of the Spirit's activity in what might be called charismatic ways (prophecy and the like) in the Old and New Testaments, so we will confine ourselves here to post-biblical history. Please note that this is not meant to be a scholarly study of charismatic history, but rather a romp through two millennia noticing that what we have today is part of what God has been doing among us since Pentecost. As the author David Middlemiss puts it: "What is called 'charismatic' in the present day is part of a long strand of apparently common experience which reaches back into the New Testament."[3] As you will notice, however, I do include extensive endnotes in order that readers who would like to take this study further can engage more fully in the subject. Conversely, if history does not interest you then you could just take my word for it and move on to the next chapter.

The "Church Fathers"

We speak of the "Church Fathers" or sometimes "the Fathers" when we refer to the earliest authoritative teachers of the Christian faith. Technically the Fathers date from before the eighth century and are those whose teaching is agreed to be orthodox according to the ancient oecumenical councils (such as Nicaea, AD 325, which agreed most of what we now have as the Nicene Creed). The list does vary, but we can think of it referring to those who gave the early agreed teaching of the church.

In *Perspectives on Charismatic Renewal*, Edward O'Connor writes that "the coming of the Holy Spirit had a powerful impact on every aspect of the church's life. The citation of the innumerable and amazingly diverse effects of the Spirit's action, which begins in the New Testament's writings, is carried forward by the Fathers of the church, especially in the Greek-speaking world, who also made the first embryonic attempts to classify them."[4]

So, for example, Basil of Caesarea, also known as Saint Basil the Great (c. 329–379), who was known for his careful leadership in shaping monasticism and caring for those without privilege or wealth, wrote that "Working of miracles and gifts of healing are through the Holy Spirit".[5]

Jean Laporte argues that "charisms are frequent in the early church, where charismatic forms of Christian life developed".[6] In support of this he considers the gift of prophecy and cites Montanism as an example, albeit a complex one. We return to this below. He warns that the "whole question of charismatic life in the early church is still very confused, not because the evidence is no good or too scarce but because scholars come to it, even today, with their own presuppositions", and we do well to heed that warning.[7]

By way of another example, Origen, a scholar originating in Alexandria also known as Origen Adamantius (c. 184–253), wrote that "traces of that Holy Spirit who appeared in the form of a dove are still preserved among Christians. They charm demons away and perform many cures and perceive certain things about the future, according to the will of the Logos."[8]

Laporte argues, helpfully I think, that three forms of charismatic life flourished in the early church:[9]

1. *Martydom* – regarded as a genuine gift of God's presence. Shocking though this might be to us it was taught that the presence of the Spirit of God might be most fully experienced in the suffering of the martyr. This can be seen explicitly in the martyrdom of Polycarp

or the Passio Felicitas et Perpetuae, the account of the martyrdom of saints Perpertua and Felicity.

2. *Didascale* – a Christian who was particularly gifted by the Spirit with wisdom and knowledge. Two examples would be Clement of Alexandria and Origen.

3. *Monastic life* – which dates from the fourth century onwards and was regarded as a calling particularly associated with the Spirit. The monastic would be visited by all sorts of spirits and be(come) practised in discerning that which was of God and that which was devilish in origin. The calling of the monk was to inhabit the spiritual world well.

There are a great many other examples of "charismatic gifts" cited in the early literature:

Both Clement of Rome and Ignatius of Antioch refer to prophetic gifts, as do the documents we refer to as the Didache and the Shepherd of Hermas. Pseudo-Barnabas also makes reference to prophetic ministry. Prophetic features are contained in the second century writing of Justin Martyr (c. 100–165) and Irenaeus of Lyons (c. 130–202). Justin Martyr mentions the reception of charismatic gifts, such as healing, foreknowledge and prophecy, and that miracles have been withdrawn from Israel and given to Christians. Irenaeus also makes mention of charismatic gifts including the discernment of spirits and exorcism, as well as the raising of the dead… Both Hippolytus of Rome (d. 236) and Tertullian of Carthage (c. 160–225) refer to healing and Tertullian notes exorcisms and gifts of revelation.[10]

Montanism

Montanism was a second-century Christian movement named after its founder, Montanus, and originating in Phrygia in Asia Minor. It held to basic tenets of orthodox Christianity, and was formed around the prophetic practice of Montanus and his two assistants. It encouraged devotion, spiritual practice, and missionary zeal but came to be regarded with suspicion and then antagonism by the wider church before finally being renounced as heretical.

It must always be remembered that "history is written by the victors", and while there were clearly concerns about the movement there have always been mixed views and there has been a notable resurgence of interest in Montanism recently. Most of the material we have comes from anti-Montanist writers so it is difficult to make accurate judgments about the movement as a whole. Eusebius (260–339) was an opponent of the movement but still describes a notorious Montanist called Quadratus "who was well known for his prophetic gifts, as well as other 'wonderful works' done through the successors to the apostles".[11]

We have already noted Laporte's argument that there is at least some good in the movement.[12] Louis Bouyer describes Montanism as the first case of a valuable and orthodox charismatic movement turning to sectarian heresy. Clearly there was value in the movement to start with; Tertullian among others was highly influenced by it, and his influence lives on even today.

Bouyer goes on, in an argument which is very helpful for those of us who would work to maintain orthodoxy alongside enthusiastic faith, to explore how heresy developed progressively. So, for example, Montanists came to regard their gifts as the only gifts and thus themselves as set apart and above all others.[13] Others who did not have such gifts and were not so ascetic were viewed as imperfect or incomplete, and thus fellowship was diminished between different parts of the body of Christ. Such absolutism and confrontationalism, which might perhaps be best called sectarianism, is often dangerous even when it is associated with valuable parts of authentic faith. A decisive element in the downfall of the movement was an erroneous but authoritative prophecy of the return of Christ: the prophecy was wrong, and the movement had little with which to defend itself. The movement died away by the sixth century but arguably, given the church's quiet but ongoing interest in the supernatural and the teachings of people like Tertullian, its influence did not completely cease.

Messalianism

Messalianism (also known as "Euchism", both names meaning "those who pray" in Syriac and Greek respectively) was a fascinating movement mainly made up of lay people which was developing between the mid-fourth century and mid-fifth century. They maintained that prayer was the only work of a monk, and true prayer is that which is accompanied by "sensible gifts of the Spirit". Once these gifts have been received nothing else is necessary, and no discipline need be observed. In particular, ecclesial structures and rites were superfluous to the one who truly prayed, and thus such a man or woman did not need the Eucharist or to resist temptation, for the spiritual man cannot sin.[14] This movement was condemned as heresy repeatedly mainly because of its downplaying of sacraments. It was finally anathematized at the oecumenical council of Ephesus (AD 431), although it continued in various forms at least up to the twelfth century.

Like Montanism, Messalianism was a movement which wielded influence beyond its immediate circle of adherents, notably including Saint Symeon the New Theologian (949–1022). Symeon argued that the gifts of Pentecost are not a thing of the past; rather "the normal development of the inner life should be... a sudden and conscious outpouring of the Spirit in us".[15] He picked up on what was, to the church authorities, a profoundly worrying aspect of Messalianism, namely an encouragement to look to those who are lay and who have experienced this powerful encounter with God by His Spirit rather than the ordained who have not. Given that they regarded their own teachers (including women, much to the dismay of their contemporaries) as reaching perfection through encounter with the Spirit of God, and contrasted these to the fallen leaders of the church, it is not surprising that this caused concern.

It is interesting to note that both of the first two post-biblical examples have been declared heretical, particularly as the next example I give was also technically heretical, and later we will see that "enthusiasm" (which was what much that we would now consider "charismatic" was called) was regarded as a thoroughly undesirable thing. It would be possible to argue either for or against their anathematization, and there are things to learn from either side of such an argument. Movements such as these seem to need to be established on or beyond the fringes of the church. As their nascent leaders look to establish a different set of priorities to the mainstream there is an inevitable distancing to allow for the new. This has great strengths and significant weaknesses.

So, to defend the mainstream church for a moment: we often see this kind of enthusiastic movement becoming reliant and then overly reliant on a particular charismatic (in both senses of the word) leader to the exclusion of others. Their devotion often seems to lead to schismatic tendencies and a growing expression of superiority. From this flows disobedience on the part of those who are under discipline and a demonizing and undermining of extant authority in more general terms. This separation leaves movements very vulnerable when new and erroneous teaching arises either accidentally or deliberately because their "own" leaders have extraordinary power.

Conversely, the mainstream church has a lot invested in its own stability, and we don't have to think very hard to come up with examples of the necessity of challenging the status quo. God cannot be "boxed" or contained, and yet at times it seems as if that is exactly what the church sets out to do. It is hardly surprising that those who challenge such structures and those who hold power within them are held in suspicion and even animosity. Charismatics, by their very devotion, will stir up strong reactions; it appears to have always been thus.

The Cathars

The Cathars are our next example or "snapshot". They "were radical dualists condemned at Orleans (1022) for advocating the consolamentum, that is, the baptism with fire and the Holy Spirit with the imposition of hands, at which the soul and the spirit reunited as the soul passed out of the power of Satan.

It was considered to be a moment of cleansing, affecting and salvation."[16] Again, history has not deemed them orthodox Christians, but it is interesting to note the parallelism to modern charismatic practice: the laying on of hands, invocation of the Spirit, and visible signs in response are key marks of charismatic practice today.

Indeed, we see these kinds of signs appearing repeatedly, marking numerous Christian leaders around the world. Although I would not argue that the following would primarily self-identify as charismatic were they alive today (such things are hard to prove), these include:

Bernard of Clairvaux (1090–1153)

Bernard was "especially known for his miracles and exorcisms" and taught that God is understood and experienced most fully beyond the mind. Thus "ecstatic contemplation [is] a gift of the Spirit... [who then] enables miracles, discernment of spirits, and godly virtues".[17] Here is remarkable, and mainstream, teaching within the church.

Hildegard of Bingen (1098–1179)

Hildegard began her monastic life aged eight having had visions from the age of five which continued throughout her life. She was a serious prophet and preacher in the church who became an abbess, which is a role with great authority and was the highest and most influential position a woman could obtain in her own right. She is known to have sung "in the Spirit" (which means that this was not an isolated part of her practice). She saw the Spirit as wind or breath, who is active in our salvation and perceivable in many ways, making us holy and distributing gifts. These gifts enabled service, victory over evil, and the performance of the miraculous. Interestingly, she also saw tears as a sign of the Spirit's presence.

Joachim of Fiore (c. 1130–1202)

Joachim was a Cistercian monk called to monastic life in a vision given to him while he was in the Holy Land and a further vision of angels bringing knowledge. Fascinatingly, Pope Clement III instructed him to write out his prophecies which, combined with the fact that he was appointed as an abbot, demonstrates that those with charismatic expressions of faith can be found within the mainstream of the church. Cartledge notes, "He is best known for his view of human history in three epochs belonging to the Father, the son and the Spirit respectively."[18] According to Joachim we live in the age of the Spirit and thus should expect to see the Spirit at work in the church. This will be an age of evangelism and will be "categorised according to the certain types of Christians (the spiritual father, contemplative men, Learned men, manual labourers, the old and weak, chaste priests and clerics, and the married and their children)".[19]

There are many others who could be cited. Mark Cartledge picks out Bonaventure, Palamas, and Cabasilas before moving on to Thomas Aquinas (1225–74), who must be one of the greatest and best known of philosophers and Christian theologians. Aquinas followed Augustine's understanding of the Spirit within the Trinity, with the Father as lover, the Son as beloved, the Spirit as love. God imparts to us His Spirit as a gift of grace, forgiving us and enabling us to participate in His life as His child. Aquinas saw the gifts of the Spirit as habits of grace. None of this is particularly remarkable, but "His early biographers recall how his sermons were accompanied by miracles and that during mass he frequently experienced ecstasy. His spirituality was expressed in hymns, especially *Almum flamen vita Mundi*."[20] This hymn (reproduced in full in the endnotes) makes interesting and edifying reading.[21]

Mysticism

This area is worthy of further study. Mysticism is an interesting parallel to charismatic experience, and there has been some fascinating work done on the overlaps between the two areas of Christian spirituality. Some parallels are spelled out by O'Connor, for example in the life of Ignatius of Loyola (1491–1556), who records experiences of all three persons of the Trinity.[22] He reflects on his engagement with the Spirit in his "Spiritual diary" and is associated with speaking and singing in tongues. There is much more work that could be done in this regard, but it is beyond the scope of this book.

Enthusiasm

As we have already noted briefly, enthusiasm is a term coined to "describe the religious fervour of the 'Anabaptistical Sect' of Nicholas Stork [or 'Storch'] of Silesia" around 1500.[23] It was a decidedly negative term that none would ascribe to themselves; it was intended to describe an irrational fanatic and used in an entirely derogatory way. So, for example, John Wesley was described, even condemned, as an enthusiast, but he himself said that "every enthusiast, then, is properly a madman".[24]

Middlemiss works through R. A. Knox's tendencies of enthusiasm,[25] a compilation which dates back to the sixteenth century, and concludes that what Knox saw of enthusiasm is very similar to much of what we see in charismatic churches today. Knox's observations concerning enthusiastic movements included:

- The movement claims to be restoring the primitive spirituality of the church.

- The movement is denounced and opposed by the mainstream churches.

- The movement becomes schismatic.

- The supernatural becomes an expected part of life.

- Total transformation of the personality is expected as the norm for followers of the movement.

- Adherents tend towards a single-minded desire to live a life of "angelic purity", which leads towards a separation from all "worldly" amusement.

- There is a desire for a restoration of religion as an affair of the heart, as opposed to the outward form of traditional religion.

- The impatience of enthusiastic grace is notable.

- A set of gifts tends to be desired which allow a direct insight into God's will, with an accompanying degrading of human reason.

- The enthusiast has a new status and authority.

- The enthusiast always hankers after theocracy.

- A group will sometimes retreat into the wilderness to set up its own society and subculture.

- There is a conviction that the second coming is shortly to be expected.

- The movement is accompanied by a host of abnormal phenomena.

I refer the interested reader to other studies of this, notably Middlemiss's work; our purpose here is served by the observation that there is significant overlap between Knox's observations of the enthusiasts and common characteristics of the charismatic movement.

The seventeenth century and Methodism

Around 1650 we see the birth of the Society of Friends, or Quakers, as they are commonly known. We might not think of them as particularly charismatic today, but their origins lie in George Fox's receipt of a vision, or more precisely hearing God's voice. Their foundation is deeply Christian, non-conformist and experiential, involving healings, prophecy, and glossolalia (as well as some degree of shaking, although this might not be where their name comes from).

Jonathan Edwards (1703–58) famously preached to great effect, and his ministry was often accompanied by outward signs, such as cries.

It is unclear what early Methodism made of what we would now call charismatic experience. Cartledge argues that John Wesley (1703–91) was sceptical, and we have already noted his comments on enthusiasm. However, as Harvey Cox explains:

what Wesley wrote about the Montanists is instructive, and by reading between his lines we can see that he had to tread carefully. He knew of reports of tongue speaking in his own day, and he – like Paul – felt more than a little ambivalent about it. Nonetheless, about Montanus he is very straightforward. Wesley described him as a "real scriptural Christian" and extolled him as "one of the best men ever upon the earth". The reason why tongue speaking and similar gifts had disappeared, Wesley said, was that "dry, formal, orthodox men" had begun to "ridicule" such gifts because they themselves did not possess them.[26]

Wesley himself records the following in his journal:

> [he] had an opportunity to talk with [George Whitfield] of those outward signs which had so often accompanied the inward work of God. I found his objections were chiefly grounded on gross misrepresentations of matter of fact. But the next day he had an opportunity of informing himself better: For no sooner had he begun (in the application of his sermon) to invite all sinners to believe in Christ, than four persons sunk down close to him, almost in the same moment. One of them lay without either sense or motion. A second trembled exceedingly. The third had strong convulsions all over his body, but made no noise, unless by groans. The fourth, equally convulsed, called upon God, with strong cries and tears. From this time, I trust, we shall all suffer God to carry on his work in the way that pleaseth Him.[27]

This is not only a "Western" phenomenon: Seraphim of Sarov (1759–1833) was a Russian Orthodox solitary monk who partially left his confinement and developed a significant healing ministry during the last eight years of his life. This ministry was profoundly informed by specific words of knowledge, while Seraphim remained orthodox in principle and practice, particularly in his use of the Jesus prayer.

At this point we arrive at the early precursors to what we would now call the Pentecostal movement. Edward Irving (1792–1834) was a Church of Scotland minister who, when serving in London around 1830, ministered over a community where speaking in tongues and prophesying were common.[28] "He is often referred to as the 'morning star of Pentecost', as speaking in tongues and prophecy occurred at his church."[29] These ideas and practices began to gain ground in a complex interplay of individuals and movements, including, in the UK, the foundation of the Keswick Convention, which proved very influential on Pentecostalism. Most famously, this led to significant revivals happening on both sides of the Atlantic at the turn of the nineteenth century. Britain saw the Welsh Revival, and Pentecostalism was born in the US.

Topeka Bible School, Kansas (1900)

These are reports from Charles Fox Parham, one of the great fathers of what was to become Pentecostalism, mostly in his own words:

> In December of 1900, we had our examination
> upon the subjects of repentance, conversion,
> consecration, sanctification, healing and the soon

coming of the Lord. We had reached in our studies
a problem. What about the second chapter of Acts?
I set the students at work studying out diligently
what was the Bible evidence of the baptism of the
Holy Ghost...

At about ten in the morning I rang the bell
calling all the students into the chapel to get their
report on the matter at hand. To my astonishment
they all had the same story, that while different
things occurred when the Pentecostal blessing fell,
the indisputable proof on each occasion was that
they spoke with other tongues... a mighty spiritual
power filled the whole school.

One Sister Agnes Ozman asked to be prayed for. Parham humbly
refused her request as he had not experienced this "filling" for
himself, but when pressed he agreed to do so:

I had scarcely repeated three dozen sentences when
a glory fell upon her, a halo seemed to surround
her head and face, and she began speaking in the
Chinese language, and was unable to speak English
for three days. When she tried to write in English...
she wrote in Chinese, copies of which we still have
in newspapers printed at that time...

Seeing this marvellous manifestation of the
restoration of Pentecostal power, we removed the
beds from a dormitory on the upper floor, and
there for two nights and three days we continued as
a school to wait upon God. We felt that God was no
respecter of persons, and what He had so graciously
poured out upon one, He would upon all.

Those three days of tarrying were wonderful days of blessings. We all got past any begging or pleading, we knew the blessing was ours with ever swelling tides of praise and thanksgiving and worship, interspersed with thanksgiving and worship we waited for the coming of the Holy Spirit.

On the night of January 3rd, I preached at the Free Methodist Church in the City of Topeka, telling them what had already happened, and that I expected upon returning the entire school to be baptized in the Holy Spirit. On returning to the school with one of the students, we ascended to the second floor, and passing down along the corridor in the upper room, heard most wonderful sounds. The door was slightly ajar, the room was lit with only coal oil lamps. As I pushed open the door I found the room was filled with a sheen of white light above the brightness of the lamps.

Twelve ministers, who were in the school of different denominations, were filled with the Holy Spirit and spoke with other tongues. Some were sitting, some still kneeling, others standing with hands upraised. There was no violent physical manifestation, though some trembled under the power of the glory that filled them.

Sister Stanley, an elderly lady, came across the room as I entered, telling me that just before I entered tongues of fire were sitting above their heads.

When I beheld the evidence of the restoration of Pentecostal power, my heart was melted in gratitude to God for what my eyes had seen... I fell to my knees behind a table unnoticed by those upon whom the power of Pentecost had fallen to pour out my heart to God in thanksgiving. All at once they began to sing, "Jesus Lover of My Soul" in at least six different languages, carrying the different parts with more angelic voice than I had ever listened to in all my life.

After praising God for some time, I asked Him for the same blessing. He distinctly made it clear to me that He raised me up and trained me to declare this mighty truth to the world, and if I was willing to stand for it, with all the persecutions, hardships, trials, slander, scandal that it would entail, He would give me the blessing. And I said, "Lord I will, if You will just give me this blessing." Right then there came a slight twist in my throat, a glory fell over me and I began to worship God in the Swedish tongue, which later changed to other languages and continued so until the morning...

No sooner was this miraculous restoration of Pentecostal power noised abroad, than we were besieged with reporters from Topeka papers, Kansas City, St Louis and many other cities sent reporters who brought with them professors of languages, foreigners, Government interpreters, and they gave the work the most crucial test. One Government interpreter claimed to have heard twenty Chinese dialects distinctly spoken in one night. All agree that the students of the college were speaking of the languages of the world, and that with proper accent and intonation. There was no chattering, jabbering, or stuttering. Each one

spoke clearly and distinctly in a foreign tongue,
with earnestness, intensity and God-given unction.
The propriety and decency of the conduct of each
member of the Bible School won the warmest
comment from many visitors.[30]

William J. Seymour, a student of Charles Parham, opened
the infamous Azusa Street Mission around 1906, from which
arose the birth of "Pentecostalism". This movement spread
around the world, not least to the UK where one Alexander
Boddy (1854–1930) was vicar of All Saints' Monkwearmouth,
Sunderland.[31] He had been shaped by the Keswick Convention
and influenced by the Welsh Revival and the holiness
movement. After his wife had been healed of asthma in 1899
he found himself wanting to engage more and more fully in
this experiential ministry and so travelled to Oslo to meet with
T. B. Barratt who was leading a revival modelled on Seymour's
work in Azusa Street. Barratt agreed to visit Sunderland in
1908, which became the centre of British Pentecostalism. It
was there that Smith Wigglesworth had hands laid on him and
was prayed for by Boddy's wife, Mary.

This is the briefest of overviews. There is much fascinating
history and others have recorded it in far more detail than I
can. I have no space to reflect on the Northumbrian saints or
the Hebridean revivals. I have largely omitted key players like
Smith Wigglesworth or movements such as the Brethren and
many others in their engagement with the miraculous. I have
also ignored such recent figures as John Wimber and David
Watson, as the focus of this chapter has been on establishing
that what we now hold precious is no new phenomenon of
the latter half of the twentieth century. No one expression of

renewal looks exactly like another, but we do see remarkable commonality of experience and expression as the people of Christ have sought to engage with the Spirit of Christ down through the ages.

The final reference I would offer you, though, is to another Grove Booklet. John Finney, in his work *Renewal as a Laboratory for Change* argues that renewal movements tend to be birthed outside the mainstream, but a significant part of them will then return and influence the whole. It is this part which has lasting significance, he, as a bishop in the Church of England, argues. God has been, and will continue to be, unwilling to be confined by the limited expectations of His people. His kingdom is coming and we are invited to be engaged in the adventure of its arrival.

Meet Roy

Roy Searle is one of the leaders of the Northumbria Community, a movement drawing on the riches of Northumbrian spirituality and some of the ancient monastic patterns, interpreted in active conversation with mission, renewal, spirituality, and worship. He writes:

"One of life's great and liberating discoveries was finding out that it was OK to be an introvert leader. I certainly need time alone to feel, think, reflect, and pray. Creative imagining and visionary leadership comes, for me, more out of solitude and silence, prayer, and pondering than through engagement and activity with others. I enjoy the interaction and engagement with people but have to find time for aloneness in order to process and reflect on conversations, experiences, and events. Self-awareness is very important to me; knowing my heart, understanding what's happening in the interior of my life is essential to my well-being before God and others and the natural source of insight, inspiration, and awareness of the Holy Spirit's promptings and activity that informs my life and ministry. As an introvert, when I do not get sufficient time alone, my spiritual equilibrium is diminished and my ability to live and lead well is challenged. I need time alone in order to be fresh, deep, innovative, resourceful, and life-giving in my ministry. Without such aloneness I can lapse into religious platitudes and empty and meaningless performance-orientated ministry.

"My energy, creativity, ability to engage with all kinds of people and be as comfortable in one-to-one situations or before a large crowd would suggest that I am quite a charismatic personality but... my spirituality? If by charismatic we mean someone who believes in the empowering charisms or gifts of the Spirit, and the transforming work of the Holy Spirit and growing Christlikeness and the fruits of His Spirit in our lives, yes, I am a charismatic. [However,] my hesitation in being described as charismatic centres around the conclusions that some people will make, that to my mind are far too narrow. I was profoundly influenced by the charismatic renewal movement in the 1980s and was baptized in the Holy Spirit during a John Wimber conference in Sheffield in 1984, an experience that released me in the gifts of the Spirit, like speaking in tongues, singing in the Spirit, and giving a word of knowledge; an experience that also confirmed my apostolic calling, that enabled me to break out of the imposed expectations of being a pastor and teacher in a local church. The freedom, confidence, assurance, and blessing that has come from that experience of the Holy Spirit has enriched my life and informed my leadership ever since.

"My concerns about being labelled charismatic are to do with a confidence that lapses into assumption and arrogance and to a casual approach to faith that belies the mystery, depth, and complexity which is part of the life of any disciple. I became disillusioned, dismayed, and angered by the hype and unrealistic rhetoric that promised much but delivered so little and was

unable to cope with failure, uncertainty, questioning, complexity, and honest doubt. I am weary of some aspects of charismatic church life: empty sentiment, self-indulgent, consumerist charismatic worship that feeds an enthusiastic subculture but makes little contribution to seeing 'God's kingdom here on earth'. As John Wimber and David Watson both used to say, 'The gifts of the Spirit are meant as tools for mission in the world, not toys for the church to play with.'

"My own experience of the dark night of the soul, which led me to appreciate other traditions of spirituality, like the contemplative stream, has also complemented my charismatic experience. Contemplation has borne the fruit of wisdom, a gift of the Spirit, in my life, and has kept my feet on the ground and delivered me from both the excesses of charismatic spirituality and guards my heart from manipulation, power plays, and the adulation, admiration, and subtle affirmation seeking that can distort and seep into the mind and life of the charismatic leader.

"If by charismatic we mean a commitment to grow in the knowledge and love of God, to deepen one's relationship with the Father, to learn, in the words of George Fox, 'to follow the light of Christ within' and to exercise the gifts of the Holy Spirit, not just in a worship service or ministry time but in ordinary life and work, I am a charismatic!

"I think of countless numbers of people within our own community, along with several monks and nuns I know, who quietly exercise charismatic ministries with little affirmation and who, because of their *vocational understanding of anonymity, shun publicity and are very hesitant about the retelling of stories – nevertheless people whom God has used to speak powerfully into others' lives, through words of knowledge, prophecy, discerning of Spirits, healing, and deliverance.*

"I think of members of the churches that I have been privileged to lead, who wouldn't speak out publicly in meetings but who would have a quiet word, often shared privately with me, which brought revelation and discernment from the Lord for a particular person or situation.

"I fear that the busy activism and noise that accompanies so much contemporary charismatic worship makes little room for truly waiting upon God in silence to hear his voice.

"In my own experience, with a real questioning and indifference to highly charged spiritual claims, where conveying something that we sense might be of God is couched in spiritual language which subtly adds weight to what we say, e.g. 'I was thinking about your situation and the Lord said...', I have nevertheless grown in confidence in trusting my intuition and 'hunches' and 'nudges' of the Holy Spirit that have informed my leadership, offering them along the lines of, 'I think the Lord may have given me a little insight... As I was praying I had this sense of...'

"I think we need to learn to appreciate the gift of both introverts and extroverts within the life and ministry of the church. Peter was no doubt an extrovert, from my

reading of his life in the Gospels and epistles, but we should remember that it was John the beloved who was the first to recognize Jesus when he appeared to his disciples on Lake Tiberius after his resurrection from the dead. The image of John the beloved, the contemplative, leaning upon the breast of Jesus, in the upper room during the Last Supper, is a powerful image of an introvert who was listening to the heartbeat of God. We do well to learn from those, often introverts, who have learned to listen, who can perceive and discern God's heart and his activity in the world."

6

Why is the Charismatic World Hard for Introverts?

S o much, then, for the terms used in the title of this study and their place in history and the Bible, but what about the basic assumption I am making, namely that introverts need help in a charismatic world or charismatics need help in an introvert world? There may be those who feel no competition between these two expressions of the self, but the common reaction to discussing this subject is that there is a perceived clash of worlds. So, in this chapter and the next, we will turn to a consideration of some of the reasons why it is hard for each to live in the other's world before looking together at why it is important that we make the effort and encourage those who are making the effort even if we are not one of them.

Please do note, however, before we go on, that not everything that an introvert finds hard about a particular expression of charismatic community will be due to the fact that they are an introvert. Some irritation will arise because of other parts of their personality; some will just occur because people are people. So, for example, charismatic culture prizes spontaneity. One of the pairings set out in MBTI distinguishes between those who plan ahead (so-called "J's") and those who leave things until the last minute (so-called "P's"). Those who fall into the "J" camp may well find spontaneous aspects of charismatic practice hard, but they could equally well be either introvert or extrovert.

I have argued that to be charismatic, in the sense in which we have been using the word, is central to being a Christian. If this is right, then, whatever shape of personality you are, there is a need to engage with what might be called charismatic, even if it is simpler at times to find another name for it.

However, the so-called "charismatic" world today has been shaped and formed in a way that can be profoundly unhelpful, at least for introverts, often for the British psyche, and perhaps for the church as a whole. I think this is self-evident, but bear with me as I make the argument. I have been pondering and discussing this subject for a number of years now, and as I have mentioned that I am wondering about writing on being "an introvert charismatic" every single person has smiled. Many have laughed, and some have stated that this is an inherent oxymoron. In our world "charismatic" means extrovert…

… except it doesn't! This is not an accurate or helpful assumption and cannot be allowed to continue unchallenged, however confident some of our friends might sound when they assert it. To accept this conflating of two quite different things is to impoverish the church and to deny half the population a significant part of their rightful inheritance and identity. The problem, though, is manifold and deeply rooted; here I want to concentrate on just two elements of it: what Susan Cain calls the "extrovert ideal", particularly within evangelicalism, and then the ways in which charismatic "culture" exacerbates this problem.

I have already referenced Susan Cain's excellent book *Quiet*, a secular best-seller which is well worth reading. One of the things she describes clearly and passionately is what she dubs "the extrovert ideal", which she says is ubiquitous at least in US culture but more widely in the West:

> The extrovert ideal is not a modern invention.
> Extraversion is in our DNA – literally, according
> to some psychologists. The trait has been found to
> be less prevalent in Asia and Africa than in Europe
> and America, whose populations descend largely
> from the migrants of the world. It makes sense, say
> these researchers, that the world travellers were
> more extroverted than those who stayed home.[1]

She traces the outworking of this in a number of settings, Harvard Business School being one of her key examples. Business and commerce are shaped by and around those who are extrovert.

What surprised me when I read her work, though, was not so much her analysis of business, but her sharp perceptiveness about the evangelical part of the church. I have already argued that charismatics do not have to be evangelical, but numerically and culturally most are and through Cain's eyes we begin to see the depth of cultural domination within which introverts find themselves, particularly because charismatic culture often seems to adopt US culture unthinkingly.

Cain arranges to meet with Adam McHugh (whose own work I also highly recommend and reference elsewhere).[2] Their conversations result in a chapter entitled "Does God love introverts? An evangelical's dilemma".

She observes the following:

... evangelical churches often make extroversion a pre-requisite of leadership, sometimes explicitly. "The priest must be... an extrovert who enthusiastically engages members and newcomers, a team player," reads an ad for a position as associate rector of a 1,400-member parish. A senior priest at another church confesses online that he has advised parishes recruiting a new rector to ask what his or her Myers-Briggs score is. "If the first letter isn't an E [for extrovert]," he tells them, "think twice... I'm sure our Lord was [an extrovert]."[3]

Reporting their conversation, she records:

"The evangelical culture ties together faithfulness with extroversion," McHugh explained. "The emphasis on community, on participating in more and more programs and events, on meeting more and more people. It's a constant tension for many introverts that they're not living that out. And in a religious world, there's more at stake when you feel that tension. It doesn't feel like 'I'm not doing as well as I'd like'. It feels like 'God isn't pleased with me.'"

From outside the evangelical community, this seems like an astonishing confession. Since when is solitude one of the Seven Deadly Sins? But to a fellow evangelical, McHugh's sense of spiritual failure would make perfect sense. Contemporary Evangelicalism says that every person you fail to meet and proselytise is another soul you might have saved. It also emphasises building community

among confirmed believers, with many churches
encouraging (or even requiring) their members to
join extracurricular groups organised around every
conceivable subject – cooking, real-estate investing,
skateboarding. So every social event McHugh left
early, every morning he spent alone, every group
he failed to join, meant wasted chances to connect
with others.[4]

After attending worship with McHugh, she describes his
response:

as if reading my mind, [he] turns to me when the
service is over. "Everything in the service involved
communication," he says with gentle exasperation.
"Greeting people, the lengthy sermon, the singing.
There was no emphasis on quiet, liturgy, ritual,
things that give you space for contemplation."...
Evangelicalism has taken the extrovert ideal to its
logical extreme, McHugh is telling us. If you don't
love Jesus out loud, then it must not be real love.[5]

This is astonishing because, while it is true, I had not realized it
was so obvious. Like McHugh and many others I feel that I am
only just beginning to realize that I am not alone in wrestling
with these things. As Westerners, we are already immersed in
an extroversion-obsessed culture. If we are evangelical we are
deeper into this mind-set as the norms of society are reinforced
with the pressure of religious expectation and both moral and
spiritual pressure to conform to the "extrovert ideal". And, as
those who treasure the fruits of the charismatic movement, it
just gets worse...

... because charismatic culture often serves to intensify the problem. I don't believe that it has to, but at the moment it does. We have reflected a little on church history and seen different "outbreaks" of the charisms of the Spirit. Elements like the monastic experience of the Spirit might well be in keeping with a more introvert personality, but they feel a long way from our current experience. We have also seen how there are many British roots to the charismatic movement we see today. However, our current understanding of, and engagement with, charismatic renewal has largely come to the UK from America. This, I know, is another generalization, but it is not an unfair one. All of the history we have considered is truly valuable, and part of the heritage we need to reclaim. However, in the popular memory it has been swamped by the revivalism and renewal of the seventies and eighties, which has swept large parts of the British church to positive and negative acclaim.

In the decades prior to this, the "things of the Spirit" were almost completely confined to Pentecostal churches of their various genres and were sidelined at best within the UK church. Alister McGrath observes that, in practice, the English church was binitarian not Trinitarian, observing that the Holy Spirit was the "Cinderella of the theological ball".[6] We are culturally drawn to the transcendence, awe, and mystery of the Father and we both receive and follow the incarnate Saviour in the person of Jesus, but we are instinctively uncomfortable with what Alison Morgan refers to as the "Wild Gospel" of the Spirit.[7] God appears dangerous once we engage with the Spirit, and we have learned, so we think, to get by without the unpredictable elements of the presence of the third person of the Trinity.

However, in the 1970s things began to change in the mainstream church, largely through the work of John Wimber. Wimber's teaching was received by significant figures in the

UK; leaders such as David Watson, David Pytches, and David MacInnes embraced his understanding and it took root in the mainstream church. Various conferences and networks began, not least New Wine (out of St Andrew's Chorleywood in the mid-eighties), Easter People, and Spring Harvest (in 1979), which have helped to transform the church. John Finney, whom I mentioned at the end of the last chapter, formerly Bishop of Pontefract (an appointment which in itself marks the immense shift in the Church of England) charts the recent history of the growth of the UK church and argues persuasively that almost every good innovation finds its roots in renewed churches.[8] He cites the Alpha Course, house-groups, healing ministry, modern music, lay ministry (beyond licensed ministry), and many other such things.

This popular revolution in the British church (no exaggeration if you consider the journey the church has taken over forty years) has looked across the Atlantic for its inspiration, in part because John Wimber was a Californian who had something that captured the British imagination. Despite his oft-repeated self-description, "just a fat man from California trying to get to heaven", he brought a gift of great value to us repressed Brits. It has been natural to continue looking in the same direction when we need help. There is much help there. The church in the US is, in places, large and thriving. There are churches of many thousands of people, and teachings abound from people with "significant", "worldwide", "ground-breaking", or any of a number of "insert-your-own-hyperbolic-descriptor" ministries. Some of these ministers are worth learning from.

Part of the issue is that the baseline culture in America is far more extrovert and outwardly confident and confrontational than we would instinctively be in the UK. Such confidence is appealing and often looks like "courage" or "faith", but it is always worth remembering that it might only be cultural or temperamental difference. We, however, are often blind to this and have tended to take on the culture alongside the wisdom and insight that is offered.

Moreover, my conversations with Gary Best have helped me understand that, in North America, this world is far more nuanced than we realize. Gary would say he was neither "charismatic" nor "renewed" because in his world those terms bring with them enormous preconceptions, the ramifications of which I am not sure I fully understand. So, for example, he would distinguish (as we would) between classical Pentecostalism and Restoration Pentecostalism, but to the North American the latter would be charismatic and the former not. To generalize, it appears that in North America "charismatics" and those "in the Renewal" would be marked by a restoration theology whereby God promises to restore in the current age that which has been lost, rather than a theology of an in-breaking kingdom set within a framework of inaugurated eschatology. They imply a high theology of anointing, whereby gifts are given to Christians to be used at their discretion rather than the authority belonging to Christ and us participating in His work. Thus, "doing what we see the Father doing" would be interpreted in practice as "doing the kind of things that we see the Father doing", rather than choosing to cooperate in work that He is already enacting.

Both of these marks would be distinct from what Wimber taught: his whole theology and practice was, in simple terms, based on making space for God to "do stuff" and then joining in. He was a long way from an authority-based impositional understanding of the ministry of the kingdom. He came to faith in the Quaker movement and almost his entire ministerial practice was based on getting out of God's way. If God didn't "show up", then "coffee's good"! If, however, God did "show up", then John and his team would be at ministry for hours and hours.

However, on this side of the pond we often don't notice this complexity and in our naivety we assume it is all one and thus we need to swallow anything that comes to us that looks "charismatic". This means that we often don't ask questions which would help us distinguish between helpful and distracting teaching, and bring us to a clearer theological standpoint from which to embrace the world and proclaim the gospel.

My developing understanding of being a charismatic has grown slowly within a vastly complex social movement which we all too often receive as necessarily being:

- loud – in actuality and in impression;

- confident – like an Englishman abroad who believes that if you speak loudly enough everyone will understand and know that you are right;

- forceful – for surely the kingdom is advancing and forceful men take hold of it; demons need to be commanded, sickness banished, and territory conquered;

- social – because God works when two or more of His people gather and it is sad for those who miss out and bad form if one chooses not to contribute the gifts one has;

- impartational – gifts are received as one anointed person lays hands on another.

I do wonder what Jesus would have made of us.

Surely the most important desire is to be more like Jesus than like another human being or culture. Is this not the place of authenticity and grace? The place of power and freedom? The place of life? The kingdom and our home?

My point, of course, is that this loud, social, highly stimulating, and dominating world is alien territory for an introvert, and is made all the more complex by feelings akin to loss or guilt which we experience when we don't enter into it fully or wholeheartedly. We can inhabit it with varying degrees of assimilation, but we will always feel that we are in a foreign land. We can wonder, we can observe, we can learn, and we can be enriched, but we will never quite be at home.

This loud place, however, is not the entirety of the charismatic world, at least in the fullest sense of this world; it is one part of it. It can be a part which sometimes thinks of itself as the whole and acts as if it is, but it is actually not. There will be many who, by their assumptions and behaviour, purport to own, dominate, understand, and shape it. It is, however, self-evidently dangerous to place faith in them or allow any individual other than Christ to shape the world according to their nature. The fact that half of us recognize this at a deep, almost instinctive, level is testimony to this: it is all right to feel this discomfort. The hard thing – and it is vital that we note and monitor this – is to honour the discomfort while valuing, respecting, and nurturing those who are inadvertently causing it.

We need, for our own health, to reclaim space to be alive and free in the power of the Spirit, and the world needs us to do just that. For the "kingdom" is a kingdom, not an empire, and the Father's yearning is that the fullness of His image is deeply ingrained throughout His kingdom.

Such an act of reclamation will not be easy. We expose in each other weaknesses as well as strengths and it is hard to face the fact that we have not got everything right or everything contained within our current understanding. Introverts will often find themselves tripping their extrovert siblings up unintentionally while being viewed as slow or awkward, and we will, or should, always find ourselves challenged to extend ourselves beyond our natural boundaries. Such growth and mutual challenge will take love, patience, and understanding. It is an act of faith, not only in the one who calls us, but also in those He calls alongside us. It is an act of virtue, of discipline, of holiness, without any of which the deeply destructive nature of the brokenness of our understanding comes piercing through the veneer of our Western "niceness". It's about faith, it's about hope, and it's about love. It's hard, but it's right, for we are called together.

Meet Ian

Ian is an experienced public leader within charismatic circles in the UK and internationally. Ian writes:

"I've always thought that I was pretty well in the centre of the introvert/extrovert spectrum but am increasingly realizing that I am probably a sociable introvert. By this I mean that I am particularly resourced and energized inwardly by pursuits which do not require the presence of other people. While I enjoy being with people, too much people time is a considerable drain upon me and while I have particular people in my life who are definitely fillers rather than drainers, nevertheless even an excess of time with them leads me to want to withdraw a little bit into my own personal space to recharge and prepare for other people time."

When thinking of spirituality, Ian reflects:

"... I relish larger, energetic gatherings and completely understand theologically and experientially the truth that Jesus is encountered especially among His people. [However] I realize that given the fact that much of my ministry is involved with people and indeed with larger gatherings from time to time, often the most precious times of hearing from the Lord and being recharged by Him come in those moments when I am able to withdraw to have time which is simply Him and me and where I am perhaps able to hear His still small voice in a more conscious way. Thus I would rather read a book than listen to a talk. Interestingly, however, I would rather pray – intercede that is – with others than by myself and probably in terms of my intercessory life am far more extrovert than introvert.

"I certainly think of myself as charismatic. For me it is hard to think of what it would mean to be Christian without being charismatic in that theologically and etymologically the word signifies the outpouring of grace upon the individual or the church and I can't conceive of a Christian faith or spirituality or experience which is not initiated by and fuelled by the grace of God. By that of course I mean that there can be no walk with God which is not initiated by God, given to us from God, by God, which is in any way independent of His activity.

"[For me,] 'Charismatic' has come to be a term which defines what I would call normal Christianity against any other perversion of it. So to define charismatic I would want to define some of the key hallmarks of what I understand to be New Testament Christianity. Thus at the heart of the charismatic experience would be an ongoing and immediate encounter with God, a continuous experience of being filled with and renewed by God's Holy Spirit, the sovereign activity of God manifested for example through the impartation of gifts of the Spirit and other Holy Spirit manifestations in the life of the believer, and worship and spirituality which touches not simply the mind but also the heart, the spirit, and the will."

In a helpful, and humorous, reflection on the tension inherent in trying to live faithfully within a complex and demanding church and world, Ian continues:

"Perhaps a further feature of the charismatic would be therefore an understanding of the spontaneous work of God and the spontaneity of Christian living and spirituality. Given the extraordinary balance which of

course I manage to capture in my own Christian walk, this spontaneity is corralled by the experience of living consciously under the authority of Scripture within the parameters of the biblical narrative and by the orderliness which the Holy Spirit also works out in the life of the believer and the church.

"I admire and warm to... introvert charismatics; thus I may well be talking about general trends and traits rather than specific stories. While not wanting to tar every extrovert charismatic with the brush of frothiness, I appreciate the depth that I see in introvert charismatics in terms of depth of encounter with God and depth of experience of the things of God. Perhaps there may be something to be written about the way in which a true and authentic experience of God and an ongoing experience of Him may lead us into more introvert ways as we dwell in His presence free from the distraction of others. Equally it may also tell the ways in which a true and authentic experience of the Holy Spirit leads to greater freedom and therefore perhaps extroversion, especially for those who perhaps feel locked into a more isolated way of living."

7

Blessings and Challenges for Charismatics in the Introvert World

One of the easy traps into which we could fall as we wrestle with the concept of "the introvert charismatic" is to assume that the only challenge is for introverts as they wrestle with engaging in a healthy manner in the charismatic world. In reality, it is just as hard for many charismatics to engage in a healthy manner in the introvert world. Not all charismatics are extrovert, but many are and both experience and teaching make us assume that introvert ways are incompatible with the "things of the Spirit". This assumption does not bear scrutiny as the Spirit often engages in reflective ways, but it is clearly seen in our frantic practice. Few charismatics would go to a prayer meeting and regard it as a dynamic success if everyone sat in silence for an hour!

We need to explore this reverse difficulty because it is not a sufficient solution for introverts to learn to cope with extroversion and slip into the charismatic world as if on a borrowed ticket. God created both introvert and extrovert and both have much to give and receive. We must learn to enable extroverts to inhabit unfamiliar places in a life-giving way. It is only in understanding the other that we can begin to reach out to them effectively. Mark Twain observed that "Travel is fatal to prejudice, bigotry, and narrow-mindedness, and many of our people need it sorely on these accounts..." Cultures differ between "introvert world" and "extrovert world", and we are invited to make travel between our cultures easier and more regular.

In this chapter I am trying to do two things, always remembering that not all charismatics are extrovert. We will end with some reflections on why this is particularly hard for extroverts, but we start with a number of common features that charismatic culture will exhibit, and consider why it will be hard for most people immersed in this culture to move easily into an introvert world.

Charismatic culture is naturally active and pragmatic

One of the most obvious things about charismatic culture is activism, which is probably inherited from the broader evangelicalism which has influenced modern renewal movements. Charismatic churches are busy places with a befuddling plethora of meetings, events, activities, and extra-curricular activities seeming to abound at every opportunity.

Within this busyness pragmatism thrives. This is natural, possibly even necessary, and produces good results in the short term. The pressing question in a busy place will often be less "Is this valuable?", and more "Is this the quickest way to get results?"

Combine this pressure with the realities of a movement which has had to carve out its own identity as it has grown from small beginnings over the last few decades, and we are left with a body of people who are active and pragmatic and who engage, whenever possible, in company. Introvert culture feels very different to this, at least to an extrovert.

Introverts need less stimulation than extroverts. We may well be active, sometimes too active, but we do not thrive on the "buzz" of mutually reinforced stress. When we are stretched we will typically quieten down, withdraw, and address the issue in whatever way we know how. This is bizarre behaviour for extroverts, who are deeply unsettled if there is no meeting called to address a problem. To an extrovert, the introverts' search for the space necessary to deal with something can appear to deny the issue's very existence.

Moreover, introverts process reflectively and, while there are many pragmatic introverts, their pragmatism cannot help but be surrounded with a degree of contemplation. This can be frustrating and unsettling for those who already "have the bit between their teeth" and want to get things done.

Charismatic culture is not very reflective

It is so easy to generalize, but one of the reasons that charismatic culture is so vulnerable to the accusation of shallowness is because contemplation is often undervalued. This is not to say that reflection is entirely absent, but whereas contemplation has been a highly prized spiritual discipline in some expressions of Christianity, this is not the case in most modern charismatic spirituality.

The trouble with this is manifold, of course, but one consequence is that the introvert world's engagement with the inner world proves uncomfortable: when we stop and look deeply at ourselves it can be an unsettling experience and we sometimes find that we do not like what we see there. It is far easier to run off and do something than it is to kneel before the Lord and honestly pray Psalm 139: "You have searched me, Lord, and you know me..."

Charismatic culture doesn't like missing out

Charismatic culture is constructed around the tangible receiving of the Spirit of God. We can experience this in many ways but our priority is engaging with what God is doing by His Spirit. This experiential dynamic at the core of charismatic spirituality is positive, driving, energizing, and good. However, it is not only good; it has other consequences. One of the main dangers is that it can lead to Christians adopting a kind of spiritual nomad syndrome, whereby they never quite settle anywhere as they are always journeying in search of the new experience.

This restlessness can be evidenced at every level: you see it in churches, for example, when people come for a while and then move on when the going gets tough or the giving becomes demanding. You see it in the songs which are universal and then abandoned, and with the preachers who happen to be popular at any particular time. Importantly for us, though, we see it socially and psychologically in the way that individual people behave. When the priority is "being in on what God is doing" and we have been taught to expect that God is experienced when we gather, it is counter-intuitive to withdraw. This uncomfortable process is made even harder when others engage in the "hype" that can appear to surround some large and emotionally intense gatherings of charismatic Christians. If I have been engaging with God silently, even if I have been wrestling with some really deep issues, and friends come bubbling out of a large meeting exuding radiant joy that "God really turned up" and "the ministry was amazing... powerful and life-changing", it takes a high degree of confidence not to feel like I have missed something. If that is true for introverts, how much more true will it be for those who are not at home in an introvert world?

Charismatic culture is not good with quiet

Quiet is an odd thing. Those of us who love it treasure it deeply and cannot understand an alternate view. For many people, however, especially in immature cultures,[1] quiet is associated with discipline and is, therefore, something that is inhabited only by necessity and under instruction. Children are told to "sit down and be quiet". Pupils are told to "work quietly". Young Christians are, or used to be, taught to have "quiet times" because they are good for you.

The world will rarely do this out of choice now. It seems that most of us surround ourselves with noise at every opportunity. We work with music on, walk with headphones in our ears, and have the radio set to start playing when the car's ignition is turned on. Quiet seems a rather unpleasant necessity, and we are not good at it.

Moreover, because we learned in our immaturity that we would be told to be quiet when we were to learn something new, there is not always a positive reaction internally to the invitation to be quiet. We suspect it might be hard work and none of us really likes being confronted with the idea that we are not good at something...

... and this is the rub: charismatics are not very good at using quiet. We are pragmatic and we like quick fruit. We like nothing more than the spiritual equivalent of Jack's beans which will sprout a beanstalk overnight and take us to exciting new places (and, I am tempted to add, even if we meet monsters as a result). We are not good at the harder, longer-term investments which take work.

We have to be honest about this core question. Those of us who inhabit the inner world recognize the fruit of things like quiet, reflection, space, and peace. Others do not find them so natural, and as we have just observed these kinds of fruits are slower growing than others.

If we really think that the introvert world has precious gifts for the charismatic we need to practise the discipline of highlighting the benefits it brings; they will not always be obvious, and that makes inhabiting this part of the world less attractive than it might, or indeed should, be. Introverts should talk about the benefits and fruits that quietness produces.

And for the extrovert...

All of this, of course, is made harder when the charismatic in question is also an extrovert. Remember that charismatic culture is dominated by extrovert practice, but is not inhabited solely by extroverts. The interaction between charismatic identity and the introvert world is hard in itself, but the more extrovert a particular person is, the harder it will be for them to engage with the positive fruits of the introvert world because there are some basic needs which they will have to set aside for a while in order to do so.

This is, of course, the exact converse of much of the argument of the rest of this book, but please do notice that an extrovert engaging in the introvert world will struggle in a number of areas:

They will miss the company of others, even if we make great efforts to give them time. Their need is often greater than our capacity, especially when other stimuli are reduced. Moreover they will struggle to know how to make the first move and engage. In their extrovert world interaction is a low-cost, low-risk exercise: I talk, you talk, everyone talks, and if it is rubbish that's not too much of a problem as something better will come along soon. An extrovert in an introvert's world will sometimes bombard those around them and occasionally realize that this is not well received. In response, some will be quiet and wait for others to make the first move: that is what would happen in their world, but this silence in introvert space is normality rather than an invitation to speak. Eventually someone will talk to them, of course, but the waiting is torturous because (it feels like) it could go on for ever! So what are the sensitive among them to do? Talking too much is apparently intrusive, but if they don't speak then maybe no one will…

Moreover, this relative peace is not only potentially lonesome for the extrovert; it also inhibits thought and response. They will lack processing space if there is not scope to do it with others. This is just as inherently frustrating for them as it is for an introvert not to be able to find space to think.

Extroverts will also struggle in a world that does not provide familiar security. An extrovert "reads" situations to find evidence to tell them how they are being received. When others are more interested in the inner life than the loudest voice in the room, this is quite unsettling. External processing leads to constant affirmation, and for such a person being asked to try something alone and internally can lead to insecurity. How do I know I have got it right? Is it worth continuing?

Furthermore, they will often feel that they are lacking information, simply because it is not given in a manner designed to cut through chatter and then explored verbally. Listening is shaped differently in an introvert world, which means that the dynamic of hearing will often be markedly different.

They will struggle with under-stimulation and often feel the need to go and "do" something simply to stimulate themselves. They will find themselves listless and needing to go in search of the things that will bring them energy.

They will find it hard to read social signs in this different social context and will often draw conclusions that are misleading. This is quite disabling for those who inhabit the outer world. I think of introvert children I know who, in certain contexts, even with people who know them well, need support when they want space. They are not (usually) rude and neither do they make a scene, but they might well slip off to read for fifteen minutes. The urge to "go and see if they are all right" is very powerful among people who care, but it is not always helpful. To an extrovert, withdrawal is a sign of malfunction, whether this is relational malfunction (you have fallen out with me), social malfunction (you are spurning me), emotional malfunction (you are upset), or psychological or even physical malfunction (something is wrong with you). The urge that will drive a caring extrovert to "sort out" an introvert who actually just wants space is profoundly disorientating when that extrovert enters introvert-dominated space.

And, of course, they will struggle at not being in the familiar situation of being in the majority. Being in a minority is usually hard, and especially so if we are not used to it.

Being a charismatic in an introvert space today is hard, then, and particularly hard for extrovert charismatics. One final dynamic makes it even harder in my repeated experience. As I have reflected on this subject with numerous people in a wide variety of contexts over a number of years I have found that almost everyone is more painfully aware of the things that they are not good at than the things that they find natural. The conversation starts with people affirming the things that are good about the type of personality that they are; however, it rarely takes long for talk to turn towards a kind of confession of feelings of guilt or insufficiency at not being "good" at the things they perceive others excel at. Introverts struggle with guilt that we don't love the things that seem to delight others. What is wrong with us? Extroverts often seem to wrestle with guilt that they cannot sit silently in the presence of God, with the Bible on their knees, and simply "be". Difficulty compounded with guilt can be really tough.

Nevertheless this is also a good place. As I argue throughout this book, but particularly in a couple of chapters' time, the introvert gifts are a vital part of the life of the kingdom of God. It is not that they will come naturally to all, but they ought to be valued by all. As we step towards them and explore we will find ourselves enriched, fulfilled, and brought towards even greater maturity in a manner which is profound and deeply healthy. Here is a fuller space, created and hallowed by God, where we can inhabit freedom and intimacy. Here is an invitation to explore wisdom and reflect on the deep things of God. Here is space to notice and to connect. Here is even fuller fullness of life and all are invited.

Meet Bishop David

David (whose name has been changed) is an Anglican bishop. Here he reflects on his "introvert charismatic spirituality":

"From my perspective Jesus is a present reality; his presence is to be experienced 'in the midst,' despite any barriers, and he breathes His Spirit into us. His powers – the powers of the kingdom, the powers of the age to come – are undiminished.

"So Scripture describes a living reality, e.g. 1 Corinthians 12, 13, 14. We are to expect these things to be true and we will experience them to be true (e.g. "in each there is a manifestation of the Spirit for the common good"). This is the way in which the church is made – by the gifts and graces of God – Christ for the world. Put it another way: things happen when we make space for Him, when we wait on Him, wait for Him, and are ready to receive from Him. Maybe that emphasis is a particularly introvert perspective? (Though it is prominent in Acts 1, of course!)

"I think of myself as an introvert. I have done the Myers-Briggs analysis a number of times and always come out 'I', though since I have been a bishop I have got closer to 'E', simply, I guess, because of the need to operate in the shadow side. My energy, however, comes from solitude and space – which of course includes Jesus since His company is within! So, I love to get back home of an evening and leave behind the chatter and conversation and be myself again. Being an introvert means that I work things out in my own

head... *in preference to working things out through a conversation with another. I guess I also tend to take any frustrations out on myself rather than dumping on others. Enough said, perhaps.*

"*Other people have described me as a charismatic or observed that I am in 'a charismatic phase'! I tend to be wary of labels. My identity arises from my parents and upbringing on the one hand and on my adoption as a child of God on the other, and I long for that to be the controlling identity. Children of God is what we are through grace; as John says what we shall be has not yet been revealed, but when He is revealed we shall be like Him, for we shall see Him as He is. But, yes, I'd identify myself with much of what I encounter as charismatic (except, perhaps the volume of the music!).*

"*I do wonder if 'charismatic' tends to be dominated by the extroverts, and, if we were prepared to make more space for or take greater account of the introverts, we would realize that the charismatic experience was much more pervasive than we thought? I was struck by the question raised by some rural (charismatic) clergy at a rural seminar I did at New Wine, which was about allowing the charismatic experience to happen in rural congregations where there might well be resistance to 'hand-waving' and 'trendy' music. I think my response was along the lines of creating more space for Jesus to do what Jesus wants to do however He wants to do it, but clearly that also means gently introducing the expectation that He will do something... the absence of a certain style of music or even the absence of a certain genre of teaching is no barrier to Jesus! Introducing the* expectation will, though, normally involve focusing on a bit of Scripture (and I think John's way of speaking of these things is especially helpful for where and how we are as church) and keeping the focus on that Scripture so that the community starts to be formed by it.

The Spirit always points us to Jesus, brings to mind the things of Jesus, and so draws us into the Father's love and will. Relationship is the heart of the matter as the kingdom is the goal of the matter – rather than the style or volume of the songs, for instance. I was going to add the raising of hands, but I think that there is an issue about our bodies being part of the offering of praise or subject to God's power. It is just that, for an introvert it doesn't come automatically – it comes, if I can put it like this, 'when you can't stop yourself'.

"So, one priest I know (an introvert) says that she lifts her hands in praise only when 'it is right' and you can do no other. One story I like: the confirmation group met after the confirmation had taken place. I asked them what had happened, what was happening for them. One woman (an introvert) said, 'Not much really, though I do find that I've started to raise my eyes when I am praying.' 'Jesus raised his eyes to heaven and prayed...' was happening for her! A newly ordained person I was speaking with last evening – again an introvert – who on outward appearances I wouldn't have described as charismatic, described being given a picture which had enabled her to see what her role was in the given situation. It was very powerful, very moving, and absolutely of God for the situation. There are, of course, instances where the extrovert is released to be still and find God inside, in the 'sound of sheer silence', and ones where the introvert is released from her interiority to find herself becoming demonstrative in worship or affection! There are lots of stories to be told of the people for whom the words of the Scripture or the liturgy suddenly become real, for example in terms of conviction of sin, or where the presence of the Other is felt. Perhaps there is something in all those stories of God graciously working with us as we are and bringing us into fresh places we wouldn't have found for ourselves."

8

Why is the Charismatic World Good for Introverts?

This is a really important question which many of us wrestle with from time to time. Why do I need to bother engaging with the charismatic world? It would be far less demanding to worship in a quiet space like a cathedral, but the basic presupposition upon which the entirety of this work is based is that there is something important going on in matters charismatic that makes it worth making the effort to engage. It won't always feel like it when, as happened the other day, we are instructed in worship to put our arms around the person next to us and jump: I have nothing against hugging people but I do prefer to know them first and hug them when it means something. However, engagement is worth the effort and this question, and this chapter, brings us back to some of the reasons why.

I have argued that to be charismatic is central to being a Christian. It's hard to read the Scriptures and not come away with the deep conviction that the God and Father of our Lord Jesus Christ is living and active in our world through

His Spirit. How can we read about the mission of Christ, and live in the embodied truth of the salvation He offers without being committed to the mission He gave us? And what is that mission but to preach the kingdom, heal the sick, and drive out demons?[1] There are things culturally about the modern popular "charismatic" church which are imperfect and sometimes even unattractive, but at its core it encapsulates something of the nature of the calling and identity of the people of Jesus in every age. I hope that this is a case I have already made, and I guess the fact that you have read this far means that you are, at least, persuaded that there is a point to be considered in this.

Moreover, I have begun to argue that the charismatic world is impoverished if it is only extrovert, as indeed it would be were it to become monochromatically introvert.[2]

What I want to argue now is simply that the charismatic world is a great place for introverts to "live, move, and have their being". We have already explored the ways in which we are taking the word "charismatic" to signify an engagement with the charisms – that is, the graces, gifts, effects, and consequences of the presence of the Spirit of God. For those who call on the name of Jesus, the Holy Spirit is not an optional extra. We have seen the basis of this in the Bible, but the Holy Spirit is more central to the Scriptures than simple doctrinal necessity. The Spirit is central from beginning to end.

God creates; we are made from the stuff of the earth, and that is entirely consonant with our modern understanding that we are "built" of the same material as the world. We have the same atoms and molecules as the soil, plants, and animals around us. Furthermore, we are knit together in the same ways as other creatures. We, too, have DNA and proteins and all the "stuff" of life. However, it was into human beings that God "breathed". He gave us of His own life, and did so by breathing, which immediately brings to mind His Spirit (Genesis 2:7). We were made in His image and it is His life we live. We were created to work and move in Him. It is only post-fall that we see God having to break into His world to engage His children in His life. How does He do that? By His word, "the word of the Lord came to me and said..."[3]; by His Spirit, "the Spirit of the Lord is on me..." (see Isaiah 61:1); and in these last days by His Son, who draws all of this together in a new covenant (Hebrews 1:2).

So Jesus comes, ministers "in the power of the Spirit",[4] sends His followers out "with authority",[5] and then teaches them to wait for the Spirit.[6] On the day of Pentecost the disciples are filled and empowered and the church is born. Those who follow are challenged, changed, baptized, and then the Spirit falls on them too. This is the pattern of the church and it extends to the next generation. So Timothy is expected to live it (2 Timothy 1:6), and the church is to eagerly desire it (1 Corinthians 12:21) and never quench it (1 Thessalonians 5:19–21). At the end of it all, it is the Spirit and the bride who say "Come!"(Revelation 22:17) and elicit the echoing call of the faithful; the true bride of Christ, His church, and the One who has been alongside and within them all the way. For at all times and in all places the people of God can proclaim with confidence "The Lord is here", and back comes the response "His Spirit is with us!"

Interestingly, though, Paul has to sort out a mess in Ephesus when he gets there in Acts 19, which indicates it is possible to miss this central facet of Christian faith.

He meets some disciples (verse 1). Note they are "disciples", in other words recognized followers of Jesus. In a world in which following Christ could bring a death penalty, you would not be known as a disciple for fun or because it was what you had always done. These were "proper" Christians.

His question to them is "Did you receive the Holy Spirit when you believed?" (verse 2), which is a great opening line. Perhaps we should use it more often ourselves, particularly when you see their response: "No, we have not even heard that there is a Holy Spirit." That could never happen today... surely.

Paul's response is to ask what baptism they received. It is the very core of their identity and faith which is in question here. Baptism is the mark of the Christian; it and the Eucharist form the central, sacramental signs of the new covenant. Paul's question probes at the heart of who they are and how they follow.

Their response is that they received John's baptism, that of repentance and faith in the coming Christ. Now it is possible to argue that they had not fully received the name of Jesus and that those who have will automatically receive the Spirit of God. I think that the point here, though, is rather more straightforward. They had confessed their sins and been washed clean. They had expressed their faith in the one who had come and was to come. Now Paul baptizes them "in the name of the Lord Jesus" (verse 5) and in an inseparable movement Paul places his hands on them, the Spirit comes on them, and they speak in tongues and prophesy (verse 6).

Entry into the name of Jesus is, in Paul's apparent practice, marked by baptism and the invocation of the Spirit marked by outward signs. Tongues and prophecy are common signs of the presence of the Spirit, but there are more. When we look at the letter that Paul wrote to the Ephesians it is riddled with the work of the Spirit. Surely he has the events of Acts 19 in mind when he writes, "When you believed, you were marked in him with a seal, the promised Holy Spirit, who is a deposit guaranteeing our inheritance until the redemption of those who are God's possession – to the praise of his glory" (Ephesians 1:13–14)? He goes on to pray for more of the Spirit (1:17), and all that implies, in the succeeding verses. The Ephesian church lived in the power of the Spirit or it would simply have limped. Like the rest of the seven churches in Revelation it either heard what the Spirit was saying or it faced judgment and death. Did they ever return to their first love and do the things they did at first (Revelation 2:4–5)? History would suggest that maybe they didn't, but the Spirit still called and spoke long after they had wandered.

To restate my point, then, to be charismatic in this biblical sense of the word, is not to be a weird or wacky Christian on the sidelines of the church; it is to be authentically and beautifully Christian. It is to follow in all the fullness of faith. It is to be alive and both work for and long for the kingdom that we pray for daily. This is true whether you are male or female, slave or free, Jew or Greek, and, yes, whether you are introvert or extrovert.

We introverts need, for our own health, to reclaim space to be alive and free in the power of the Spirit, and the world needs us to do just that. Truthfully, we cannot do this by ourselves and we need both grace and wisdom in order that we can learn from our extrovert siblings in Christ and remind them that they need us: the richness of the image of God can most fully be reflected in humanity when we unite in all our difference and choose the path of cooperation and fellowship.

I have already argued, of course, that this will not always be an easy process. Difference can be exhilarating and creative, but equally it can irritate and elicit prejudice. This is one of the reasons why it is so important to notice differences, for it is only as we appreciate the rich diversity of gifts given to the people of God that we begin to take the difficult choice to move beyond our immediate preference and embrace others. As this choice becomes consistent we often find ourselves discovering riches which were always present but previously hidden. The Psalmist writes, "How good and pleasant it is when God's people live together in unity... For there the Lord bestows his blessing" (Psalm 133). God's blessing is always found in this place of deliberate unity, for this is how He orders His creation.

Why, then, do introverts need to engage with the charismatic world?

God created all things well and because introverts belong in His kingdom they have much to give and a significant part to play. They also have much to receive and in which they need to grow. We humans have been designed and created to be better together and, like it or not, introvert and extrovert need each other.

In particular, several areas seem apparent which illustrate introverts' need of those who are more extrovert than they are and the importance of sustaining a culture in which all can thrive.

Introverts need to move beyond themselves

Introverts process things internally and are usually at home in their own company. They ponder and wrestle and conclude and face the world with confidence... but not necessarily wisdom or depth. One of the issues for them is that, although it is true that introverts are not automatically self-absorbed or socially inadequate people, they still can lack external reference points if they are not careful. This can be a profound, wonderful, and creative thing, and very often leads to a right dissatisfaction with easy answers; but the reverse side of this particular coin is that there are times when introverts find themselves creating the world in their own image and thus keeping themselves out of touch with the fundamental reality in which they live.

We all need to inhabit the world into which we are born, and especially those of us who follow Christ. He created us as part of a body, which means we both need and are needed by other parts of that body. Moreover He sends us into the world to love it, witness to it, and show the mark of the kingdom within its darkness and despair.

Introverts can struggle with this at times, as they may well feel misheard, overlooked, frustrated, and sometimes even snubbed. However, healthy relationships with the whole church of the kind we will talk about later are vital if we are to give as well as receive. When introverts are loved they will find themselves drawn out, and in many such situations people will struggle to know who is introvert and who extrovert. Active belonging is especially vital for those who struggle to feel they belong.

Introverts need faith that is bigger than their horizons

I think it was Mark Twain who said "God made man in His image, and man has been repaying the favour ever since." We all limit God by sticking Him and His work into boxes of our own making. One of the unseen wonders of the church is the way that others acting in love can take our blinkers off; we cannot do it for ourselves and remain ignorant of our spiritual tunnel vision when left to our own devices. One of the key gifts that we give to each other in our difference is the gift of breadth and perspective. This is particularly true when we, who are limited in our humanity, seek to worship and witness to the limitless God.

I am, though, particularly conscious of this for introverts. They are just as subject to the temptation to make God fit their understanding as the next person, but they tend to process things by themselves, or in smaller groups with those who are more likely to agree with them. Introverts need those who will push them and stretch them. We all need people who see bigger or who see differently. Our faith is faith in the One who is utterly beyond, and if we are to keep that faith as genuine faith (rather than a spurious hope of our own creation) we must be those who are an active, contributing, and receiving part of the body.

Why do I say contributing? It is important because one of the characteristic temptations for introverts is that, after trying to contribute to a conversation and failing to do so because others are pushing their views harder than they can, they listen and quietly sit in judgment, believing that we know better. Occasionally they might actually have better knowledge or understanding, especially if they have delved deeply into the matter in hand while their extrovert siblings are processing like mad in the conversation of which they wish they could be part. However, when we judge others we find ourselves with logs in our eyes (Matthew 7:3) not just blinkers, and healing is required… healing and, of course, the help of others if the log is to be removed.

Just a note here, which really belongs in chapter 10, but while we are on the subject: this process of not joining in debate can be a vicious circle if we are not careful. Imagine the scenario in which a group begin to discuss something which an introvert has previously considered. The introvert may try to get into the conversation, all the time continuing to process internally while others throw ideas around and develop them "on the table". Eventually, in some frustration, the introvert tosses their fully formed conclusion into the ring, often with some paucity of grace. This stops the conversation because people either have to agree or take apart something that has clearly been carefully considered. This can have the twin effect of both the introvert seeming aloof or arrogant and also making others wary of letting them into a conversation again because they seem to "dive-bomb it" when they do contribute. Introverts need to learn to contribute with questions and half-ideas that engage in the conversation. More of this, however, later.

Introverts need to give away what God gives them

This is important because they have valuable things to offer. Extroverts do need to include quiet people, but introverts need to meet them halfway. We are part of the body together, and that means that we need to work at it together.

When we are hurt or frustrated, therefore, as we will be at times, taking our bat home is not an option. To do that is to take away a gift that Jesus has given to His bride, and that is not our prerogative. This will mean that introverts need to develop their voice, but it also means that we all need to develop in communities. It is communities which contain many of the gifts of the kingdom, communities where these things are developed in practice not just in theory, communities which can communicate the gifts of the quietest, newest, or shyest person with confidence and clear testimony. We need to be together if we are to share what God has given us, and that we must.

Introverts need fellowship, perspective, encouragement, and discomfort

Finally, introverts need to be in the charismatic world because they have all the needs that any other human has. We all need healing and loving. We need correcting, rebuking, teaching, and training in righteousness. We also need discomfort: this is not an argument for any of us to have everything our way. (That would be absurd, not least because no two introverts have the same likes and dislikes, but also because we are all fallen and need to be stretched and guided.) Engaging with Christ and His church is not comfortable, but there is room here for all.

There are gifts we receive in community, particularly in charismatic (in the sense I have tried to develop) community, which is earnestly seeking the in-breaking of the kingdom of God. What place could we long for more? Here we find gifts of belonging, victory, progress, rescue, love, joy, and peace. Here we find the blessing of the body.

The charismatic world, then, is hard at times, but it is still where we need to be. Later we will take this further and consider how we can thrive and grow as introvert charismatics, but we also need to remember that we are not simply enjoying the hospitality of those who create a charismatic world. Our more introverted space is also a deep gift when we can invite other charismatics into it. It will be a strange place for them. Indeed at times it will be a stranger place for them than their world is for us because culturally they are used to having things their own way; however, it is a very important gift that introverts have to nurture, develop, and give away.

A Letter to Introverts from a Charismatic Among You

My dear introvert friends,

I write as a charismatic among you; one who has often moved beyond our shared comfort zone and found great blessing there. I write as one who has come to appreciate the abilities of my less introverted charismatic friends, and who sometimes suffers what the missionaries used to refer to as "reverse culture shock" at times when among those of a more reflective nature. I write as one who is convinced that the two worlds we are discussing need not be in competition, but who also recognizes that we often find ourselves in a place which feels like it is subject to undue pressures from others around us. Hard though this is, I have also come to see that we can be our own worst enemies at times, and this letter is intended as an honest reflection upon our need to play the part that Christ created us to inhabit within His body.

Introversion is not a disability. If anything it is an ability, although it is not really that either: it is a preference, a shaping, a part of the gift that is you. It does not define you, limit you, or predetermine you. It is simply a way you prefer to operate. It is precious, good, and to be treasured.

You have so much to give, but please remember that the rest of the world does not know what you are thinking, or indeed whether you are thinking at all. Western society is dominated, numerically, behaviourally, and culturally, by those who think out loud, who process externally and verbally.[1] What seems obvious to you in a conversation will often be hidden from others unless you speak it aloud. This is not necessarily because you are clever, but because introverts will often reflect before a conversation or silently withdraw within it and ponder while others talk. They think within the conversation, and your thoughts only add to theirs as you engage. Your conclusions may be right or wrong, valid or invalid, constructive or irrelevant (and it is worth remembering this), but others will not have taken the same journey as you have and will not see things as you do. Extrovert insights are formed in the open for all to debate; your silent wisdom will only be explored if you invite people to do so.

Moreover, others may need help to follow your train of thought, not because they are stupid but because they will have been thinking their own thoughts and concentrating on the conversation. Our extrovert siblings will almost always need help to understand that what you are presenting is more than a thought along the way. You might have thought very carefully before you spoke but you will be heard by a world which is accustomed to people chattering their way through even the most vital of decision-making processes. This means that we need to "show our working", as they used to say in maths at school. This is hard for us because we naturally prefer to work things out internally either alone or in a safe space with few others. In the charismatic world we are often drawn into a place where processing is shared in a group and your thinking, logic, or conclusions will not remain unscathed when offered to the discussion. What has been neatly worked through will be shaped by others in a manner which can be surprisingly distressing.

This does mean that we need to try to hold conclusions lightly until they are actually reached, and to give ourselves permission to take something away and ponder it. Sometimes it will lead to you feeling like you are repeating something that you said earlier in a conversation because earlier it was just taken as a passing thought but actually it was far more than that. It will entail you learning not to react too quickly to something that others are about to reject; just because it has been said does not mean it is yet believed. It also means, though, that you are excellent checks and balances to "group think". Many a time I have witnessed a group leading itself to a conclusion which is not properly considered, only to be rescued by the introvert who has not really contributed except to ask the question of whether we are sure that this is what we really believe. Now beware: this does not make us immediately popular! Others may well feel as if we had the answer all along, or are playing some kind of game with the group. This kind of wisdom needs great care in the offering, but it is a precious gift you can give, particularly to a group that trusts you and each other.

Please notice, though, that the fact that you are instinctively quieter than others and your verbal offerings are usually more composed will often lead to misunderstanding.

On the one hand, lazy, ambitious, or busy groups will be tempted to overlook you. They shouldn't, but there are only so many times people will remember to draw you in. The responsibility for addressing this lies with each *of us. Learning how to contribute is really important because the reason you are overlooked will rarely, in my experience, be that people don't want to hear.*

On the other hand, your quietness may well make people uneasy, strange though this might appear to those of us who live in the complex reality of an introvert world. Our quietness can give people a variety of negative impressions. Some will see us as withdrawn and needing help. Others will see us as rude or superior and aloof. Some will regard us as all-knowing and will find themselves wary around us. In an extrovert world that derives at least some of its security in the observing or overhearing of the thoughts of others, the opaque box of an introvert's life can be unsettling.

This might all sound frightfully intrusive; allowing others into your thought processes can be challenging, but there is one part of this that does bring some considerable freedom. You can be far freer than you will instinctively understand to make mistakes in what you say. For an introvert it is a terrible thing to have spoken in a way that later we regret. We will tend to treat our words as an expression of our self; we process and then communicate. It is as if our speaking is the offering of a conclusion upon which we can now be examined, but the world we inhabit does not treat most words like this. Words are simply interaction. They might be right or wrong; their value is in the instant and measured by sincerity. They can be moved on from, not because they are valueless but because they are one stage in a longer development of an idea.

You may well have words from your past which "haunt you" for reasons that you cannot quite understand; their power is remarkable, whether they were spoken by you or by others. There can be many reasons for this, of course, but one of them lies here. People do not hang on your every word, and you needn't either. Moreover, the words that people speak over you are rarely the final communication that they want to give. For us words are tangible expressions of considered reality. Today's Western world uses words as disposable cartons conveniently housing the fast-food of shallow communication, needing only to be sturdy enough to be tidy but disposable immediately after use. Grasping this permission to let go of many words, to leave them behind and forget them, brings remarkable liberty.

Thus there are many reasons that we need to engage healthily beyond our preferences. Unless we choose the life of the hermit, we will be forced to but the challenge is to do so in a way that is constructive. There is much to be given and received. We need this and we are needed.

This is important because everyone needs to be drawn, at times, into the inner world. Some will see this, others will resist it, but it is necessary for all who seek spiritual health. What we tend not to spot is that each of us worries about the bits of spiritual life we are not good at. Introverts feel guilty at not engaging as fully as others, but many extroverts are hampered by great feelings of inadequacy at not being able to be quiet and reflective. Many describe a real hunger to be with God but genuine fear because quiet is oppressive and hard. Somewhat bizarrely, one of the most helpful ways of enabling this is by engagement with those who are natural in it and an almost tangible "hand-holding" in the quieter place.

Thus we model the importance of the inner world, and we keep the hunger for it alive. We are different to the prevailing norm around us. We are not better or superior as others might fear. Neither are we inferior or worthless as we might fear. We are complementary, different, necessary, and as special as others. We are called upon to live good practice, and with care we can become those who are skilled at guiding others into that place of reflection, peace, and spacious prayerfulness. The church needs this gift and the fact that God has created a world with introverts as an essential part of it would imply that the kingdom of God needs introverts, and needs us to be introverts within it.

Finally, please can I encourage you in two directions at the same time. You need to be kind to yourself, and let's not use our introversion as an excuse for not engaging with others. This is really hard because there will be plenty of times when what you need is to withdraw in order that you can recharge your batteries, but just as we might be tempted to observe that some of those who are a little impaired in the hearing department will occasionally use their real disability as a convenient excuse for not hearing something, those of us who need space can succumb to the temptation to choose it just because it is nicer.

Introverts can, and will need to, build relationships and spend time with others. We can engage in group work, and sometimes that will be what we need to do for the greater good. Introversion is not a disability; it is a gift which can be used in a variety of ways, and when we use it to shape the world to our own preferences we begin to build resentment rather than acceptance.

It is vital that we develop the self-awareness to recognize our own limitations and needs. We must regulate activity and engagement so that we can be healthy, energetic, wholehearted, and committed... but please don't wave the introvert card as if it is a joker in the game of social interaction.

Let's learn to offer this fantastic gift with which we have been blessed. A friend of mine observes, probably not originally but certainly memorably, that what most people need is a "jolly good listening to". You can do that. You have the gift of attention and when you learn to give it, it can be gratefully received in a manner which is extraordinarily transformative.

It is time for introverts to step out of disguise, out of the shadows, and play our quiet part for the sake of the world, the kingdom, and each other.

With deep affection,

Your charismatic friend

9

What do Introverts Offer the Charismatic World?

As we have seen, the charismatic world is a place in which introverts can (and should) belong and we can be grateful for all who have gone before and all that we have been given through their lives. There is much that each of us needs to learn and practise, and we have reflected upon some of the disciplines with which our extrovert siblings bless us. However, there is much that introverts need to offer; much that is precious that arises out of the people the Lord created introverts to be. I am, however, entering dangerous territory here, for what I am about to say must, of necessity, be a generalization. Here I am merely describing common gifts among introverts, and not implying that they are gifts every introvert has or that no extrovert will ever have. We are all unique and all have individual strengths and weaknesses. Here, though, are some of the common gifts that introverts treasure, and gifts that they should be in the business of sharing.

This caution is important to note because generalizations can emasculate the power of the analysis they are intended to convey. If we observe that men can't multi-task as well as women can we are in danger of either assuming all women are excellent multi-taskers or that there isn't a man who can multi-task. This, in turn, can be oppressive to the woman who does better when doing one thing at a time and close the door to the opposite kind of man. However, if understood as a generalization it can be helpful when considering how women and men tend to approach tasks. So it is with these reflections. You will find reflective extroverts, and lots of wise ones. Some introverts will not listen well. However, here is food for thought, some insights into general behaviour, and some reflections on the kind of gifts on offer.

So, with that caveat, what do introverts have to give?

Introverts offer a familiarity with, and comfort in, the inner world

This is, perhaps, the defining characteristic of an introvert. They are energized by the inner world. If an extrovert child is whispering at the back of the classroom he is not necessarily simply being disobedient; he may well be waking up, engaging, energizing, and coming alive. For the introverted child, their escape is into a daydream.

The inner world is, for them, a place of joy and freedom. It is a playground full of adventure, mystery, discovery, and peace. It is a land they know well and a place where they can meet God and explore the mysteries of His kingdom. There are some inherently dangerous temptations here if this is left unshaped, but it is in itself a very rich thing. It leads to a depth of engagement and transformation which is profound for the individual and can also be for others if it is able to be shared in community.

Introvert charismatics who discipline themselves in prayer search the deep things of the Word and the Spirit and engage with them personally. They search for holiness and integrity. They face the questions of life with frankness, openness, and honesty and find in their brokenness a place of healing. In probing their own inner weakness they can be on a journey to discovering the sufficiency of the grace of God. They bring deep hope of being known by God, knowing themselves, and, if they are in community, of being known by others, although this will often be a cautious and lengthy journey.

This characteristic can, if both parties will learn to communicate with and value each other, be offered as a lovely gift of grace to the whole community. None of us can survive in just the outer or the inner world.

Introverts offer the practice of reflection

The introvert is one who will ponder and reflect. They are like the wild animal who grabs a bone and withdraws to chew while the pack engage in the communal frenzy of the next hunt. Much is observed in community, but most of it is explored and learned in the quiet place.

It is noticeable that Jesus' pattern is often, as in Luke 4, that He engages powerfully with the brokenness of this world and then withdraws to a quiet place.[1] I am (still) not saying that Jesus was an introvert; all I am observing in making this point is that both activity and reflection, noise and quiet, are vital to the One who is the new Adam.

So the introvert brings reflection to the charismatic party. They are, it must be said, sometimes received with a little irritation when they do this; but more often, in the long run, they are valued because of the fruit they bring. They ask questions because that is how they inhabit an issue. There are times when they need to let go and get on with things, but the questions still matter and those who are predisposed to notice them need time and space to reflect and share the fruit of that engagement. To introverts, they are not a distraction from the matter in hand; they are, to a greater or lesser extent, the issue.

Introverts offer the space to wrestle, question, ponder, and wonder

The introvert, then, is a wrestler. That is what happens in the quiet place. Here is pondering and noticing, processing and formulating, wondering and delight. The inner world is not divorced, or at least shouldn't be divorced, from the outer. It is part of a continuum.

This is introvert practice and with care it is a great gift, both in the fruit and the process that is shared with others. Apparently many preachers are introverts. That might sound odd, but in the pulpit an introvert can take that which s/he has explored and, in an environment which is non-invasive, can present the treasure s/he has found. Here are gifts.

More than that, though, the practised occupant of space has both the privilege and the responsibility of helping others to find space. We all need it in different ways and at different times. Both mystery and depth are essential dynamics in the life of the Spirit and it is the calling of the Christian to inhabit both certainty and wonder.

Introverts offer the dignity of space

This internal process of reflection and engagement needs space, which means that introverts also are able to curate space for others. This space is a thing of great beauty and precious dignity.

Humans are created in the image of God, not in the image of another human being. One of the hardest things, I think, about ministry is learning and practising this. We constantly want to give people what *we* have got and get them doing as *we* do. Succumbing to this urge gives us a sense of worth, in part because it draws people into treating us as they should only treat God: they are giving us worship, worth-ship. This will not do!

True pastoral ministry draws others into the presence of God and creates the space for God to deal with His children, but this can only happen when one child is prepared to step back and respect the humanity of the other. The minister of the gospel is to be like a butler in the Lord's household, never the master of the house. It is their role to order and protect that domestic space in a manner such that the master's work can be done and His will enacted. It is this "butler-ing" that I mean by "curating" space for God and others; it is His will, work, and way, not ours. Introverts are just as prone to make the world in their own image as anyone else, and there are times when they need to be more "hands on" than they would like to be, but one of the gifts they can bring is the determination to protect space for the weak, wounded, vulnerable, and unsure so that they can be fully human and in deep and direct relationship with their Father.

Introverts offer the gifts of listening and noticing

When I was going through the process of being selected for ordained ministry in the Church of England I was told that I should find a "spiritual director". I was linked up with a wise older Christian who would talk with me and recommend helpful books. Later, having moved, I needed to find someone else, and I remember approaching a leading evangelical for help. I sat in his study for an hour as he talked at me despite barely knowing me. I never went back.

The Revd Canon Robert Warren, who is a vastly experienced minister and writer within the Church of England, often says that "what most people need is a jolly good listening to", and he is right. Too often we offer care by just talking at people and it rarely helps. Adam McHugh observes that one of the gifts introverts bring is "Spiritual Direction". They like to engage on a personal level: to pay attention. They listen and notice. Admittedly there are times they need to be willing to offer what they notice rather than simply holding it, but it is a gift they can share and in which they can grow.

Moreover, as Christian leaders, introverts can shape communities into groups which notice and listen. Bizarrely, I think there is a valid argument that says that introvert leadership of a community gives rise to a more outward-looking group than the stereotyped "successful" community of extroversion which does many good things and then celebrates them in a manner that unwittingly draws all the attention back in on itself.

Introverts offer a hunger for the heart of God

It is often said that "like attracts like" and that we "look for what we know". These are clichés because they have more than a grain of truth in them. Often those who inhabit and explore the quiet places of the soul hunger for the deep things of the Father. They long for His heart, His nature, the depth of His being. They are not satisfied simply with the work of His hands, wonderful though that is. The paraphernalia of the spiritual gifts are great, but they are only the tip of the iceberg. In the quiet place there is communion with the One who is over all and in all, the One who was and who is and who is to come.

Here is the heart of worship: the glory of His presence and the beauty of His love.

Introverts will not always excel at practising the presence of God, to borrow a phrase, but the yearning is there and it is deeply precious and not to be abandoned with the coming of the next "big thing". All of us are easily distracted; a wise community will not only recognize what is important, but also those who hold on to it.

Introverts offer the search for wisdom

Perhaps most importantly for me, introverts have within them a yearning for wisdom. I think this is the gift I hunger for more than any other, and I have done since I was a boy. It seems inexplicable to me that this is not the central desire of every Christian. Why is this not the gift that we preach on and practise most of all gifts? We recognize it and revere it in a few, but mostly we ignore it, favouring instead the passing delights of the new and the innovative.

Wisdom is that deep and applied knowledge of the ways of God. It is the holding of the Creator's hand and understanding the beating of the heart of creation. It is the mind of Christ and the living application of truth. Wisdom is speaking with the accent of the Father and seeing from the perspective of a child hoisted on His shoulders. Wisdom understands and probes understanding. Wisdom makes knowledge look like an impatient upstart and delights in the nature of being.

There is an important point to be made here, though: wisdom in the Bible is never, as far as I can see, a personal gift, in the sense that it is given for one person alone. It is a gift given through one or more people for a community. When Solomon asks for it in 2 Chronicles 1:10–11, this is what he asks: "Give me wisdom and knowledge, that I may lead this people, for who is able to govern this great people of yours?" And God replies, "… since you [have asked] for wisdom and knowledge to govern my people over whom I have made you king…"

Wisdom illustrates perfectly that introversion is a strand within character, not permission to withdraw from community. We belong with the family and our distinctive gifts are just as vital to it as the gifts brought by any other, as too are the challenges that are brought by the family to each of us, whatever our personality may be.

Wisdom is precious, and when faith can find security out of the limelight it can be nurtured. However, wisdom doesn't flourish in the glare of immediacy. It, even she, is precious and yet elusive.[2] Developing wisdom takes time and desire, yearning and discipline. It is to be cherished where it is found.

I wrote earlier that "To accept this assumption [that 'charismatic' is 'extrovert'] is to impoverish the church and to deny half the population a significant part of their current inheritance and identity." The church is poorer without introverts, who have much to learn, but also have much to give. Introverts belong, in all senses, to the body of Christ.

Meet Aian

Aian is a young Christian minister, recently emerged from theological training and engaged in local church ministry in an urban context.

"I grew up in an Anglican church that had some connection to John Wimber and the vineyard movement in the eighties. When we moved church in my early teenage years it was to a church from which the youth group travelled two or three times a year to Soul Survivor Watford as well as to the 'Soul Survivor' summer festival. Charismatic spirituality has always been part of my Christian culture. I enjoyed worship, but as a teenager found it easier to manage the overhead projector, to help the band set up, and to help with the sound desk. When I was part of the congregation I would often find myself praying for the people around me or reflecting on the words of the songs rather than 'losing myself' in the worship.

"By the time I was eighteen I found myself in what felt like a conflicted position. I had a year in which I had been very involved with my church. I'd set up and run a Christian Union at my sixth form college, I was enjoying a really close walk with God, and some 'thorns in the flesh' seem to have been removed. I spent most of my day in church on a Sunday, but I felt increasingly wary of some of the 'charismatic worship' that the church ran. Sometimes you could see the Holy Spirit moving powerfully, but at other times, while people were closing their eyes and raising their hands as the band began to play, it seemed an automatic, one could even say

religious, reaction, rather than a spontaneous response to the Spirit. Then, dare I say it, there were even occasions where I felt that the atmosphere had been created through hype, lighting, music, etc. It confused me at the time that people seemed able to have their religious experience regardless of what God was doing. I realized that people of all faiths are capable of having religious experiences; what I deeply wanted was to meet with God. So, if I am honest, part of my experience of being both an introvert and a charismatic has been to go through a time of scepticism of the experience created by collective worship.

"I spent the next decade in churches that did not have the background, inclination, or resources to be charismatic. During the first five of these years I did feel very dry in my own spirit, yet still on occasion would feel led in a particular direction. I still trusted that God was at hand. I began to explore a call to ordained ministry which necessitated a move back to the Anglican Church. My new home was not more charismatic than my last but there was openness to reviewing the worship of the church. As someone with some of the skills, musically at least, for this I unexpectedly found myself to be a 'worship leader'. In hindsight this was perhaps the beginning of a road firmly back to my charismatic heartland.

"Skipping forward five years, as I was looking around theological colleges some of the old questions still remained; in fact, one college did not feel like the right place to me precisely because I was uncomfortable with the automatic/religious nature of their 'charismatic' *worship. However, I was back in a place where I wanted to see the gifts of the Spirit manifested my life: gifts of discernment, healing, and teaching are examples of those that I believe I am meant to practise, not by my own inclination but because of what God bestows. I am sure that I was led to attend the college that I eventually did.*

"As I trained and experienced different church traditions I found myself comfortable in and indeed often longing for silence. I've enjoyed the use of incense, and have found works by Brother Lawrence, St John of the Cross, St Ignatius, the life of St Cuthbert, and others to have resonance. I was also immersed deeply in the Bible and I found within me an emotional passion (perhaps not matched by cognitive ability) for hermeneutics.[1] And at the root of hermeneutics I found that the Bible must be understood as the book of the church, and as the book of the Spirit. There is no Christian quest for the word of God in the pages of the Bible apart from an understanding both of the Spirit's inspiration and illumination. At the end of all these roads I have found the Holy Spirit.

"The same sense of God with me as peace, which I carried through three years of being severely ill as a teenager, the sense of joy that I received when I was signed with ashes[2] at the age of eleven (coincidentally also when I first knew I was called to ordained ministry), have been deepened and enriched. I have seen an increase in both my comfort and experience of tongues as I pray without words. I have received pictures and interpretations for events and places of

which I knew nothing until after. It has been quite a precious few years.

"What does any of this have to do with being an introvert? In the revival movement I think that there has been very right emphasis on collective worship, on the practice of praising God. When you say the word 'charismatic' I think many people automatically think of a style of worship. If spirituality were left to the introvert alone, the world would be a poorer place. But having established a vibrant pattern of worship in the charismatic movement, it is the place perhaps of the introvert to be the friendly critic, to keep the movement honest to seeking the God, Father, and Son, who breathe out the Holy Spirit on the church. There is the danger in any 'religion' that it comes to rely on its methods. God is not brought by methods but He is willing and has promised to be found by the people who seek Him. I have come to see that worship should be a multisensory event – our Father has made us multisensory people. There is nothing wrong with the candle or stage lighting, with incense or with bubble machines, with plainsong or the big band onstage – nothing wrong with any of it in its own right, but it requires people with discernment to keep testing, so that our 'worship event' is all turned to the purpose of worshipping God and not just to the creation of an event. A worship leader or team or event points the way but must then step aside, directing all of itself to the Love of God."

10

Six Steps Towards Fullness of Life

I hope that, by now, you will be fully persuaded that introverts belong in, and are essential to, the life of a healthy church that is seeking the fullness of the kingdom of God.

If you are introvert, my prayer is that you will have been receiving permission to be the introvert you were created to be. This does not mean that you can have everything your own way; you are still a sinner who will get things wrong. It does mean, though, that you have not been "wired wrong" and you have tremendous gifts to offer.

If you are an extrovert, I pray that you have glimpsed that there is something precious here which needs to be sought, cherished, encouraged, and released. I hope, too, that you have glimpsed the attractive invitation which beckons you to be part of the rich life on offer here.

And if you are an "ambivert", as many people will feel that they are, I hope this exploration has given you hope and scope to explore part of you that really matters.

These truths and hopes, however, do not automatically make

it easy for introverts to live in a charismatic community, and it is to this tension that we must now turn our minds as we draw towards a conclusion.

What can introverts do to survive and thrive? How can they offer themselves in a way which is helpful? What strategies can be employed, what techniques learned which will equip them to be the body parts they are called to be? Here are six top tips which I have found helpful in different ways. They are not exhaustive and neither are they magic. I am simply wandering a little way down some paths that I have found useful; I am taking you on some small excursions with the hope that you will find landmarks and ideas to enable your own exploration to be more adventurous and more confident. I am, however, all too aware that in this, as in so many territories, I am a fellow explorer reclaiming native territory rather than a practised guide.

1. Recognize and accept that you are an introvert

Recognizing and accepting that you are introverted, or at least have introvert dynamics within you, is not only the first step in (re-)engaging with our church and world; it is also often enough to enable the whole process. Introversion is not a box into which you can either be placed or place yourself. It does not define you or limit you; it is simply a trait within your personality which inclines you in certain directions. Understanding and accepting yourself allows you to bring what you have to a world in need, because in this deeply personal sense you can only offer what you have if you are who you are. Many of the reasons for this are obvious, but let me spell out some of the more immediately apparent implications.

Jesus picks up the teaching of Leviticus and tells us that we should love others as we love ourselves.[1] Some have taken this to teach that we should love ourselves, and while that has always seemed an exegetical stretch it is certainly clear that there is an assumption that we will. God has made us, and He has made us well, and it is not narcissism to recognize this. To love someone will mean we value them, believe in them, make space for them, invest in them, forgive them, and cherish them. All of these are things that we are called to do for ourselves just as we do for others, and for others just as we do for ourselves. To do otherwise is to refuse to love one whom God has not only created but one whom He loves more than we can imagine. I think of a young man I know struggling because his wife was being really hard on herself. He describes finding words to explain to her that he felt she was belittling and refusing to forgive one whom he loved more than any other human being in the world and this was hurting him. They both described it as opening a whole vista of life. We do well to think of the look in the Father's eyes when we start beating ourselves up about something. Listen again to some words from Psalm 139, interpreted here by Eugene Peterson in *The Message*:

> Oh yes, you shaped me first inside, then out;
>   you formed me in my mother's womb.
> I thank you, High God – you're breathtaking!
>   Body and soul, I am marvellously made!
> I worship in adoration – what a creation!
> You know me inside and out, you know every
>   bone in my body;
> You know exactly how I was made, bit by bit, how
>   I was sculpted from nothing into something.
> Like an open book, you watched me grow from

conception to birth; all the stages of my life
were spread out before you,
The days of my life all prepared before I'd even
lived one day.

(Psalm 139:13–16, *The Message*)

Furthermore, when we accept ourselves, others find it much easier to love us. This can be taken too far, of course, but I am not talking about narcissism or self-obsession. We are invited to be at peace with ourselves, to accept who we have been created to be, and in this others find a language with which they can engage with us. It is difficult comfortably to know someone who does not know themselves.

Moreover, in accepting ourselves, we start making space to be who we are. This is vital for those who need space simply to survive mentally and spiritually. If introverts don't accept their introversion they will assume that they are like others and end up frustrated by their apparent shortcomings. Recognition and acceptance, however, enable exploration of whole landscapes of wonder which were previously simply refuges to which they retreated in weariness, confusion, and even shame.

In this exploration the inestimable value of the internal dynamic of life is rediscovered. Once we value something we usually start to recommend it to others, and usually it is received with gratitude for it is inherently precious. Our self-knowledge can bring life and freedom to others as well as to us. It reshapes community and enriches the people of God. Far from narcissism or self-obsession, when held before Christ right self-knowledge becomes a profound act of humility and worship. We are His children and His creation. What brings greater joy to a parent than a child who is peaceful, joyful, loving, and growing in health, morally, spiritually, physically, and mentally? What brings greater delight to a creator than the creation functioning well? Our growing maturity and self-knowledge, while always having the potential to turn to idolatry if it becomes self-obsession or selfishness, is part of the sacrifice of praise we offer to the One who shapes us and calls us into freedom and life.

Myers-Briggs and other material that opens up questions of personality typing are real gifts if they give language with which to explore the self. They can be oppressive and constraining when used to define and confine, but when used as a springboard this new language releases permission where we may never have had it, to simply be who we were designed to be. It is not a weakness to be quiet or reserved. All that we are can be either a strength or a weakness simply depending on how it is used. The question for an introvert is, to use a different metaphor, not why I am such a bad hammer. It is whether I am willing to be happy being an excellent screwdriver... and quietly get on with inserting screws while others enthusiastically attack the nails.

2. Learn the disciplines that feed you

Alongside self-acceptance we also need discipline – discipline to learn what is helpful and healthy and discipline to develop and practise good habits.

Let me give you a personal example: if I get up and spend time in quiet in the still of the morning, praying, reading the Bible, looking through the diary, and reflecting, then the day often seems to "go well". I approach things with energy. I have patience. I care about things. I am able to bite my tongue. I have, in other words, space for others in my day. If I miss out on the devotional space then the day often seems a struggle. I am sure this is partly about God's grace at work, partly about getting things in the right order, and partly just about how I am approaching the day, but the pattern seems clear. However, knowing this does not make it easy to leap joyfully and energetically out of bed and search for my Bible.

This illustrates the two observations key to this "step". Firstly, we must recognize what "feeds us", and secondly we must discipline ourselves to "eat". In terms of discipline we will often find we are on our own. The modern church does not excel in encouraging each other in spiritual disciplines in practical ways, although actually being accountable for our spiritual practices is immensely helpful. Whether this accountability comes from a relationship with a small group of fellow Christians, or a house group, a cell group, or a spiritual director, doesn't really matter, as long as it works – by which I mean it genuinely has a good and lastingly healthy effect for you (rather than simply looking or sounding good).

When we consider what kinds of things feed us, we should always be on the lookout for fresh ingredients. Our basic diet needs to be balanced, but it should also be fresh and healthy. Some of the key habits appear to be rhythm, relationships, and boundaries.

Rhythms matter for introverts; we do not thrive on chaos. I have already mentioned the start of the day, but they run throughout it. It is not that there is *one* right rhythm; it is that rhythm and routine seem to be important to introverts. It is fun, but tiring, to constantly have to work out new ways of doing things. There is evidence, for example, that we sleep better if we have a "bedtime routine". Rhythms are bigger than that though. They can involve public worship, meeting with small groups, engaging in quiet times of prayer, biblical reflection, and praise,

177

but the general point is that we need to spend time discerning what will enliven us and build it into a pattern that creates space and sustains.

These spaces give introverts the energy to interact and engage. Many public introverts find that most people would not know they were introverts. Those that know them well would, and some key clues will be apparent, such as, for example, a preference to work on their own; or their dread of being given a complex task which an un-led and undifferentiated group must analyse, tackle, and complete together. However many, if not most, people they meet would not really know. They have energy and social skills because they have developed healthy rhythms.

Alongside the rhythms, boundaries are very important. Let me give you another example from my own experience. My role involves pastoral work. I have come to learn that this is highly valuable but deeply draining. I put one hour in my diary for pastoral meetings and with firm subtlety build the expectation that we will engage in this kind of formal conversation for as long as is necessary but we will do so in one-hour chunks. I do this because I can pay close attention for about an hour. I can listen and pray, or listen two-ways, for an hour. Beyond that I fade with alarming rapidity. My mind wanders, my attention drifts, and my heart begins to complain. It is not that I stop caring about the person; it is that my emotional muscles give up. It is far better, therefore, to recognize this beforehand and set boundaries of life and health. Others may not realize I am doing it, but it is essential if I am truly to care for them. Furthermore I try not to programme more than two such engagements in any one day. I will break them up by some time to study or write sermons, time to deal with e-mail, or whatever. I set boundaries.

Boundaries which are wisely established will mean that introverts can thrive in public. We can enjoy meeting new people and lead demanding and complex gatherings. We can "be the life and soul of the party" at times, and engage wholeheartedly in social contexts. All these things are possible because we are released and nurtured by inhabiting safe and nourishing space.

Boundaries really matter. So, for example, phone use needs to be disciplined, particularly mobile phones. E-mail and social media cannot be allowed to intrude on everything. Family time especially needs to be created and protected. Children, in particular (whether extrovert or introvert), need to see in practice that they are important and loved, especially if as a family you are going to learn to make times when the house will be quiet.[2]

Moreover, both rhythms and boundaries can act like rewards. Most of us, given that we live in an extroverted world, need to find ways of urging ourselves on. Just as runners will tell themselves that they will "just get to the top of this hill", so we can use space as an encouragement for ourselves. We know that we will be exhausted by something but it is all right because afterwards there are things in place which will revive and sustain us. (Incidentally, this is also true of, and important for, our extrovert friends when it comes to wrestling with the quiet disciplines of the heart which are vital for all of us, but which come more easily to some than to others.)

The final habit that I will highlight here, although there are many others, is the discernment of relationships that will feed you. This is not to say that you won't (or, indeed, shouldn't) have relationships which don't feed you. We don't love people for what we get from them. Indeed, one of our core disciplines is that of service, where we give without counting the cost. However, in terms of survival and self-care you need to be alert to that which feeds you. Where do you find others who make you laugh and with whom you can cry? Where are you loved? Where can you explore your ponderings and know that they will be valued and enhanced? For introverts, such relationships are usually found in smaller settings. Healthy Christian leaders, a surprising proportion of whom are introvert, are usually part of smaller prayerful groups of some sort and often find them the mainstay through the challenges of ministry.

Friends matter, although being popular doesn't really. As we find ways to allow others to accompany us on our journey we find strength and wisdom and companionship.

3. Find a voice

This third step picks up on a theme which I was developing in the first. We are part of the body of Christ. We have, and we embody, things which are essential to the well-being of that body, and those things will find expression in one way or another. In my observation this either happens well or it bursts out in ways which are unhealthy both to the "blurter" and the "blurtee". We must find constructive ways to offer who we are.

Please don't hear this, though, in too extrovert or even too word-based a way. To say that you need to "find a voice" is not meant to imply that you need to become talkative or dominant; it is simply a metaphor to encourage you to find places, times, and ways to express that which is inside, to "speak out" that which has been entrusted to you. I speak of "words" and "speech" because there is something central to our humanity which is profoundly word-y. We were created with a word. We are redeemed by the Living Word. The core of our communication is with words. Words matter and are part of the mystery of loving grace between us as people and between God and us.

We don't need to become people of many words, and neither should we assume that the words of the quiet are somehow more valuable than those of the voluble. Introverts must not presume to be the sole custodians of wisdom or hold others to ransom until they give a fair hearing. As I wrote the very first draft of this text I was on sabbatical in a monastery reflecting on a rule of life. The third chapter of the rule of St Benedict contains these words:

> As often as any weighty matters have to be debated
> in the monastery, let the Abbot call together all
> the Brethren, and himself declare what is the point
> under deliberation. Having heard their counsel, let
> him prudently weigh it with himself, and then do
> what he shall judge most expedient. The reason why
> we ordain that all be called to Council, is because
> the Lord often revealeth to the younger what is
> best. And let the Brethren give their advice with all
> subjection and humility, and presume not stiffly to
> defend their own opinion, but rather leave it to the
> discretion of the Abbot; and what he shall think
> more expedient, to that, let them all submit; for, as
> it becometh the disciples to obey their master, so
> doth it behove the master to dispose all things with
> forethought and justice.
>
> ... If any matters of less moment have to be
> done for the benefit of the monastery, let him
> take counsel with the seniors only, as it is written:
> "Do all things with counsel, and thou shalt not
> afterwards repent thee of it."[3]

What is interesting and pertinent here is the value that is placed on the counsel of the whole community. All, even the youngest, are valued and it is only on matters of least import that the Abbot can act with the limited wisdom of the senior brethren.

If this is true in the monastic setting then it is equally valid in modern expressions of the body of Christ. We have a responsibility to listen together and to listen to each other, and each of us individually has a coterminous responsibility to learn to speak and, moreover, be willing to make the first move in doing so.

We will discuss ways of doing that verbally, but first let's observe three vital truths about this "voice" that we must find.

It must, firstly, be *authentic*: it must be you speaking. It will take from the deep things within and give them life in the community of faith. Two authentic words are far more valuable to the kingdom of heaven than a thousand words expressed for show or effect. Note that such authenticity is marked by the integrity of the speaker, not by the reception of the community. They don't have to be right, they certainly don't have to be perfect, but they do have to be real.

Secondly, notice that you *don't have to say much*. McHugh notes something that I have observed as a gift not uncommon among introverts – that they will in a few words pin down a conversation that has been dancing around an issue for much time. To learn to speak does not necessitate learning to be talkative.

Thirdly, notice that some of the most powerful communication is *non-verbal*. I think of people whose words are written, or cooked, or in cards, or with flowers. The cry of their heart is heard in dance or music or poetry. Words do not have to be spontaneous to be heartfelt and real. This is about expressing the life you share with the Father in the freedom of the Spirit. It is a gift to you and through you to others.

4. Learn a second language

It is important to discover a voice, but there is a further step that all can take and some will find they must take: this is to learn a second language. I am talking about what I call "extrovert speak". It is not a beautiful, precise, elegant, or concise language, at least to my ear, but it is the language of much of the world and speaking it opens all manner of doors.

I know that this is an incomplete metaphor, but it is one worth considering. Many of the world's problems, from those within a marriage to those between nations are prolonged, exacerbated, and sometimes even caused by people misunderstanding each other. It is said that the United States and Great Britain are "two nations divided by a common language": from the comedy of being invited by a church leader in South Carolina to "come shagging"[4] with him and his family, to the frustrating fact that "to get cross" sounds "cute" to the American ear; we say one thing and are heard to say another. In marriage counselling the underlying activity is often no more than to enable one party to hear the other. Indeed Gary Chapman's excellent book, *The Five Love Languages*, uses this metaphor to help countless couples each year learn to love each other better and more naturally.

Extrovert-speak is all around us all the time. While it will never become an introvert's mother tongue, all benefit when introverts learn how to speak it and hear it. There are things that can be said far better using it, and some things that native speakers will struggle to hear unless others speak in language, metaphor, and methodology which they understand. Often introverts and extroverts use exactly the same words just (sometimes) in a different manner. We need to learn how our words are heard and when there are better ways to express those things we wish to say.

Let me give you a couple of examples so that, even if the metaphor is lost on you, you can reflect a little on what I am saying.

I mentioned earlier that introverts tend to give birth to fully formed ideas and that this can be difficult for extroverts who need some outward processing time to engage with the new thoughts, and for introverts whose word-babies are mauled and reshaped when they should be cherished. This means that introverts can give people the idea that they are not really engaging with what others bring to a conversation. They can appear to present a fully formed proposal from which they will not then move. In actuality, they are simply presenting their thinking in so far as they have done it, which has involved far more thought and internal debate than would be the case for an extrovert, simply because introvert processing is mainly internal, in preparation for what others say. Introvert processing of others' input is, largely, subsequent to the conversation, whereas extroverts will be busily processing within the conversation. Both sets of ideas move on, but it can looks as if introverts are not engaging in the conversation because their position is not apparently developing with every twist in the discussion.

One possible response to this is simply to follow an argument through. This can feel like it turns conversation into an academic exercise without integrity because we are simply engaging in an "if-that-then-this" rational process rather than being persuaded and actually changing our minds. However, three things can happen. The first is that the mind will catch up with the intellect (although I am not quite happy with those two words). What I mean is that as we subsequently process what has been said, we may very well come to the same conclusion internally if the intellectual process has been careful and rigorous. The second is that introverts need to be careful not to commit themselves before they have had time to reflect because they need to understand in their native language too. Thirdly, though, and of greater significance, I have found that by speaking "extrovert-speak" I can be blessed with the wisdom and experience of my extrovert friends and interlocutors precisely because the conversation draws their insights out; this is of great value.

When an introvert is able to commit what, to them, is a half-formed thought into a trusted conversation they can begin to develop the confidence to explore more of those thoughts in contexts where they will be developed. It is not simply that you bless others by speaking in their language; you too will be blessed and enriched.

This is true not just of words or thoughts. One of the things it took me a long time to realize is that people, perhaps especially extroverts, don't instinctively trust that they are being listened to. (Bizarrely we do trust that we are being understood when people seem to be listening which is a far greater leap of faith, but that is another topic.) Introverts may well recognize the situation of being told they are not listening only for them to recite the last few minutes of the conversation to demonstrate that they are. Recently I said the same thing to a child and evoked exactly that response; they were listening in "introvert". Extrovert listening usually involves external processing, and signs of this are inadvertently given. You know you are being heard by an extrovert because you can see it. I had not realized I, too, was looking for these signs; I am so used to living in an extrovert world!

So, when I talk with people now, I try to listen sufficiently in "extrovert" to let people know they are heard. My listening is peppered with all sorts of unnecessary (to me) paraphernalia: "I see!", "Right!", "Really?", and "OK" abound. On occasions when I don't feel I understand I will ask something like "Are you saying..." and this genuine question is usually received with surprise and then a half smile, as if someone is surprised to be interrupted and then pleased that they are being actively listened to. Even the distracting interjections seem to encourage speech. At its best this is extrovert listening combined with introvert attention.

There is more, though: introverts will never be totally native in an extrovert world but it is false to assume that extroverts do not want to listen. The question can be as simple as how an introvert breaks into a conversation. One useful technique here is what I call "stopping words". A conversation will be buzzing from thing to thing and there is something important that you want to say. It is too complex to blurt out without care but you can say something like "Hang on a second here..." and usually friends or colleagues will stop and listen. They create the space into which you are then empowered to speak. They don't do it unwillingly but they may well not have noticed that something was brewing if you have no way of letting them know. Another technique is to phrase observations as questions so that they don't sound like an attempted closure of the discussion, and a more complex and developed thought can be fed into a wider debate.

Such techniques, of course, come far more naturally as you grow in confidence. They develop as you partner, sometimes intentionally, with extrovert and introvert friends alike and learn to communicate. Our growing confidence draws us out and draws us together, but there is one final extrovert-speak trick which we need to learn if we are to engage.

Introverts need to learn to let things go. Words are not always as permanent for extroverts as they are for introverts. Extrovert words can be spoken, used, and discarded as steps on a thought-journey, whereas for an introvert they are far more akin to the description of the destination of a journey. Once you engage in extrovert-speak you will find that you say things which are not right or even of which you are ashamed. If you are to be healthy you will have to learn to accept that this is OK – at least it is OK once you have apologized and sorted out any consequences. Others forget far more easily than you will, but you have to let them go too. It is the price of communication, and will probably never mean that you just throw words about, but any foreign language student needs to be willing to make mistakes.

5. Step out in faith

It is hard in a text like this not to overgeneralize in places. However, it is generally true that introverts and extroverts try things out in different ways. Extroverts work things through in public. I don't think that they like to look foolish any more than the rest of us, but foolishness looks different from different perspectives. To one it is stupid to try something that will clearly fail, while to others it is silly to refuse to look for a solution to a problem which matters. An introvert, in general, will look to work things out in private and then implement them publicly once they have been tested.

Introverts tend to prefer situations which are predictable and even controllable, although that control is exercised in a very different way to extrovert influence: introvert influence is often exercised more by observation and reflective response to the input of others than by the projection of personality or will either directly or in the shaping of debate. This is another example, though, of our exploration being bigger than the debate between introverts and extroverts and it is important to remember this. Those who are "J" on the MBTI spectrum prefer to know beforehand what is going to happen, whereas a "P" is generally happy to go with the flow. An "I-P" might be far happier with chaos than an "E-J", but in general introverts don't like surprises that force them to be a certain way with others. A surprised extrovert will have far more resilient natural "tools" to respond externally in an appropriate way. A surprised introvert needs either to withdraw or to process the surprise in a second and less natural "language".

This can be profoundly difficult in a spiritual setting. God longs for His children to grow and to step out in faith. Sometimes this will be very public and sometimes it will be quietly, but all of us are called to move forward. The fact that this is so often expressed in extrovert speech and action does not negate its necessity.

Let me give you an example. Often in Christian meetings we will be asked to respond publically in a time of ministry. We will be asked to stand or put hands up or come forward. Indeed sometimes when people pray for others there are the most extraordinary phenomena which might glorify God but they certainly draw attention to the one being prayed for. Many introverts express feelings of discomfort in that kind of setting. Who is really going to stand up when the Spirit apparently prompts the minister to ask anyone with genital warts to respond? And yet people do...

Nevertheless, it is vital that we all learn how to respond when the Spirit speaks. We may well, and perhaps for our own sanity we should, shy away from jumping up and down at every opportunity, but we still need to seek prayer and engage in the call of the One who loves us.

I have a friend who refuses to dominate and control ministry time when he leads it in meetings. He reports being accused of being a coward and "not stepping into his gifting" by charismatic colleagues. Time after time he will simply wait and allow God to do what He is going to do, and usually there are some remarkable things that happen... the bold thing to do is to let God take the lead and not know what is going to happen. It is far harder to wait than to follow a formula! However we do need to be prepared to step out.

In particular, we need to be pushing ourselves to step out in spiritual gifts. We face a spiritual battle and there will always be pressure not to use that which God gives us. Our calling as those who follow Christ is to use the gifts He has given us, and to use them in a manner which cooperates with what He is doing. This is a matter both of discipline and growing delight, as we refuse the temptation to use our gifts in a self-gratifying way, but always to keep in step with the Spirit (Galatians 5:25) and choose the path of service and cooperation.

So let me ask you, presuming that you are reading this as an introvert:

- Where are you beyond your own control and in the realm of faith?

- Where do you practise stepping out?

- Who will you trust enough to help you discern your gifts and begin to use them?

- Who has the authority to push you beyond your comfort zone?

- What are your spiritual gifts? How do you know? Are you using them?

- What do you hunger for and long to see God doing around you?

There is no one right way to do any of these things, but they are important areas in which all of us can grow.

6. Practise the habits that bring health

One of my former church leaders used often to say that we should "pray as we can, not as we can't". There is great wisdom here which links to our need to invest in the things that feed us, and to develop a balanced diet. Two mistakes we can make are to allow ourselves to become unhealthy either because we continually eat that which we can't digest or because we live on fast-food. Neither will do; we need to learn to be healthy in our spiritual lives.

What, then, makes for a healthy spiritual life? I make use of a metaphorical framework which refers back to physical fitness, not least because the physical is so often a picture of the spiritual in the Bible. If we are to be healthy there are seven things that our bodies need. We need oxygen, we need good food, we need to drink, we need to take exercise, and we need to get rid of waste. Sixthly, and remembering that the Bible says we are part of the body rather than being the whole body, we need to be in working relationship with the rest of the body; a healthy hand is part of a healthy arm and so on. Finally, we need wisdom and good judgment to bring all of this together. We can be as health-conscious as we like but if we make unwise choices we will not thrive.

So I ask myself the following set of questions, taking my seven needs and observations almost in reverse order.

Am I in genuine fellowship with other believers?

This is what I am called to in Christ and it is often a significant indicator of spiritual health. As a teacher of the faith I worry about those I meet who are not regularly part of a worshipping body. It is a myth which often leads to serious self-deception to believe that we can thrive on our own.

Fellowship will look different for each of us and for many introverts will be on a smaller and more intimate scale than for others, but it is vital. It is illustrated by the following questions:

- Who am I caring for and being cared for by within the church?

- Who is challenging me and praying for me?

- Whose burdens do I share and is this helping?

- Where am I exercising my gifts within the body?

- To whom do I turn for help and counsel?

Am I confessing my sins and moving on?

Just as the body needs to get rid of waste, so the Christian needs to let go of sin and be washed clean. We are broken and we all sin and the heart of the gospel is that Jesus forgives us. That, however, is a relational transaction not a spiritual standing order which we can set up and then forget. Each of us needs to let go and receive forgiveness and then grow.

So we might ask:

- Where and when do I "examine my heart" with the Lord (see Psalm 139)?

- How am I growing in receiving forgiveness?

- Where do I need to forgive someone?

- Is this dynamic part of my prayer life?

Am I exercising spiritually?

Am I taking the nourishment of my faith and putting it to good effect? Am I finding those I can serve and putting effort into doing so? Notice that exercise often only feels like exercise when we start doing it, but it is still necessary to continue. I remember when I broke my leg and then tried to stand on it once it came out of the plaster. The leg simply gave way and it was hard work to learn to walk again. Now I rarely have to think about how to walk. So it is with service. Sometimes it hurts, often we hardly notice, but the question is whether we are doing it, because if we are not then things will wither and die.

So I use the following questions:

- Where has my faith been evident to others in my actions today?

- Whose life, especially those beyond the church, would be poorer if I wasn't here tomorrow?

- What am I working at getting better at for the sake of another?

Am I drinking enough?

I think of drinking spiritually as contemplation and prayerfulness. This might seem obtuse, but I think of learning things as food and relating to God in conversation as drink – the fluid and dynamic side of my devotional life. This is simply a metaphor, but I find it helpful. Our faith is both static and dynamic, and so we need to spend time in conversation, both speaking and listening, with the Lord. This is refreshing and often enjoyable. It brings life and health and new direction. I need to pray not as I can't but as I can. I search out ways to be with Him that are natural even if they are stretching. Thus I will ask:

- Have I found space today to bring my life and my concerns to the Lord?

- How much time have I spent listening?

- What have I noticed in these conversations?

- What have I simply left with Him for now?

- What have I become aware of Him specifically handing back to me for particular attention?

- Are there words, Bible verses, people, or situations of which I am particularly conscious and I need to carry in my heart today?

Am I eating well?

Just as we need to spend fluid time with the One who loves us more than we will ever grasp, so we need to feed on His word and His goodness. Bible study is not just for new Christians and neither is it simply what we get on Sundays. There are so many ways of studying and countless books, CDs, and internet resources that will help us. We just need to create space and we will find that eating is a very pleasing thing indeed. Sometimes it feels to me that, spiritually, we eat so little that we are forced to take medicine that gives us the impression that all food tastes disgusting. A healthy diet, though, can be delicious as well as nutritious.

- What bit of the Bible am I reading at the moment?

- What can I remember from it?

- How does it fit into the bigger picture?

- What has the Lord said to me today through it?

- Is there anything I am feeling I should share from it?

Am I breathing?

Too often we get so immersed in the current world that we feel we need to hold our breath and not breathe the air of heaven. Again, you might find the metaphor odd, but we need to spend time with the Father, time simply "in the Spirit", time alongside Jesus. John wrote, "On the Lord's Day I was in the Spirit, and I heard behind me..." not because he was showing off but because this is what we do (Revelation 1:10). We need to rest in the embrace of the Father. We need to stop, to be still and know that He is God.

- When did I last know the embrace of the Father?

- Where and when do I stop?

- Do I value the place of peace?

- Is there a still centre where I can be "in the Spirit" in my life?

Am I hungry for wisdom?

Here we come round full circle. I boldly affirmed earlier that introverts search for wisdom and I think that we do. However, we need to practise. This is what holds it all together, and we need to learn how to do this both by getting it right and by growing through getting it wrong. "We have the mind of Christ", but we need to discover how to listen and think with it (1 Corinthians 2:16).

So I wrestle with questions like:

- What would Jesus say in this situation?

- How would I react if my thoughts on this issue were projected on a public screen?

- What is our long-term aim in this situation?

- What does the Bible say about what we face?

- How is love best expressed here?

- Have I prayed about this?

- Am I looking expectantly for God to move here?

In all of this there is a great invitation to walk with Jesus in the pathways of this world and bring healing, deliverance, forgiveness, and salvation. This ministry and grace are not ours; they are His. It is the Spirit who convicts and heals and we are invited to cooperate whatever our personality or inclination. As introverts we need discipline and we need to learn to step out in partnership, but here we find the greatest invitation of our lives: the invitation to life in all its fullness.

Meet Kate

Kate Bruce is an Anglican priest and Deputy Warden and tutor in preaching at Cranmer Hall, Durham. She writes:

"I was fascinated when my colleague Mark started to talk about the concept of the introverted charismatic. Lots of lights went on and I found myself making strong connections between my understanding of the charismatic and my experience of silent contemplation.

"In many ways I live my life as an extrovert, happy to throw myself into the busyness and intensity of community life in a theological college. However, the older I have become the more I have realized that I have to retreat regularly and I find solitude more and more appealing, and increasingly necessary if I am to function well.

"I realized that I may not be quite the extrovert I thought when some years ago I went away on a week's silent retreat. I was worried that the silence would be too much. How could I survive without opening my big mouth? I needn't have worried. I found myself energized by being alone and deeply contented within myself. My awareness of God in all things was sharpened and my inner life seemed to ignite into a riot of imaginative creativity deeply connected to prayer.

"I think I have, up until relatively recently, seen the term 'introverted' as negative. There was a time when if I had played the word association game I would have linked extroversion with words like 'energy', 'fun', 'sociability', and 'laughter'. Extroversion would conjure up the bold and bright colours: red, orange, and yellow. Extroverts were the shiny, happy people. Introversion, in contrast, I secretly labelled, as 'dull' and 'tedious' and coloured in with grey and blue. For this I apologize unreservedly and eat all my words along with a large side salad of mistaken assumptions. Recognizing my own introversion, through the experience of silent retreats and time spent alone, has blown my prejudice apart. My introverted self needs space to drop down into the deep places of silence and stillness – which are far from grey in colour and not in any way dull or tedious. My introversion causes me to stop and enter into the contemplation of God which is kaleidoscopic with wonder and colour and energy.

"Connecting with God in a way which might be described as 'introverted' might be misrepresented as self-indulgent: 'me and my God' alone, full stop. In reality there is no 'full stop'. In the practices of spiritual contemplation there is a searching for the gifts of discernment and openness to the prophetic word. Here I have found rich resources not simply for myself, but material which has fed into the preaching and teaching work I have been able to offer in my local church, to the wider church, and in the theological college where I work. In a similar way my experiences of contemplative engagement with God have been profoundly healing personally which in turn shapes and informs my pastoral work and work in spiritual direction, not least because my 'stuff' doesn't get in the way. The fruits of contemplative engagement with God, the work of the introverted charismatic, naturally flow outward into the church and wider society.

"To be honest, until recently I associated the term 'charismatic' wholly with a particular style of worship, one which I rarely feel moved to embody, and which in its very public intensity can really make me squirm internally. However, if, as I am now convinced, 'charismatic' means being aware of and open to God the Holy Spirit then there seems to me to be a direct link between spiritual contemplation, seen in such practices as Ignatian prayer and lectio divina, and being charismatic. I had confused one expression of openness to the Holy Spirit – 'charismatic worship' – with all expressions of such openness and concluded that the charismatic is not for me. This is a fundamental category error, which is theologically inaccurate and spiritually damaging. All Christians are necessarily called to be charismatic as a response to the Trinitarian nature of God. Shunning the charismatic effectively means denying the present reality of the work of the Spirit; we become binitarian not Trinitarian. Realizing that I have made a category error in my understanding of the term charismatic frees me up spiritually to be myself with God. I can understand myself as charismatic in my approach to God without feeling obliged to wave my hands in worship, or favour a particular musical style. I can be 'quietly charismatic'. I can be myself."

11

Towards Some Resources

I n the hazy days of planning this book, this final chapter was to be some kind of collection of worship resources which would be life-transforming, energizing, challenging, and deeply refreshing to your average introvert charismatic…

… but, of course, now I get to it I realize the danger of lazy assumptions even when you have spent a lot of time thinking about something or someone. There is no such thing as "your average introvert charismatic". We are not all alike and there is no one act of worship, study technique, or evangelism trick which will suit everybody at every time, or even that will suit any individual at all times and seasons of life.

Moreover, I have not been able to find much material out there, and I have been looking, which is crafted for introvert charismatic worship. In part, I am sure that this is because introverts can be part of any activity in the church; however, it would be good to gather material which is particularly helpful. It would be good if, together, we could begin to address this and so we have created a website (www.introvertcharismatic. org) which has a growing number of links and space for people to send in good material and sources of exploration, as well as discussing what is already there. Please do consider contributing to this as it would be great to be able to resource each other and even better if we could enrich the worship and mission of the whole church through our contributions.

However, there are a number of things that we do need to take seriously, and ask others to take seriously, if we are going to shape the corporate life of the church in a way which nourishes and releases introvert charismatics and enriches others who need to drink from this fountain from time to time. In this chapter I will begin by making reference to some general sources of good material to help us in this. More importantly, we will then move on to consider ways to make any activity more accessible for introverts while continuing to be fully open to the Spirit. This, longer, second section is where we will end, and this is important: we who are blessed with the gift of introversion are both invited and called to engage with the full range of what God is doing in His church and His world today. There are no "no-go" areas for introverts, even though some environments are harder for us. We can learn, grow, and thrive in most situations, and there are few situations in which we cannot be of benefit.

Some resource areas for introvert charismatics

There are a number of areas for which it will be helpful to think about specific resources that will be a blessing to the introvert. As I say, the work here is only just beginning, but let's at least nod in some of the right directions.

Introvert evangelism

Perhaps this is the most obvious area, apart from worship, where introverts will struggle. We are not exempt from the work of evangelism and witness, but this is hard… the models in common use in the church are not ones that leave us jumping for joy or raring to go. Few introverts, however enthusiastic we are for the Lord, will relish the thought of approaching strangers and "sharing faith" with them.

This, however, is not the only way to share faith. As long ago as 1980 Rebecca Manley Pippert wrote about introvert evangelists in her excellent book *Out of the Saltshaker and into the World*.[1] The key, she says, is to find ways to initiate conversations in contexts that give us a chance to respond as human to human.

One of the ways we sought to engage in evangelism in my last parish was through laying on a city-wide festival based on the scarecrow festivals you may have seen in rural areas, particularly in the north. We ran two "Angel Festivals" in order to engage with families, businesses, schools, and individuals and draw them into a conversation which continued in many unforeseen ways.[2] The aim was to spark people's imagination, provide something fun and intriguing, and enable creative dialogue between church and community. It was great to see all types of people able to find their own space to engage, and to shape that conversation around "the message angels bring".

We do need to move beyond the "introverts make good hosts" which I have read so often. Some introverts will, but many have more to give. I hope that I have established by now that introverts are often very good with people, which means that they have an essential role as evangelists. Indeed an introvert with deep questions may well find themselves more engaged by an introvert evangelist than an extrovert one who wrestles with such questions in a very different manner. An introvert will wrestle and care and ponder long after the extrovert has moved on to a rather more engaging "target".

The question is not, then, how introverts can do their duty and survive the experience of evangelism; it is rather how they can engage with those who are interested in faith in ways that are sustainable and life-giving (literally in this case).

Introvert pastoral work

Pastoral work is often thought of as the mainstay of ministry in the local church. We do, of course, need to be careful about what we mean by "pastoral work", as too often we find ourselves veering worryingly towards ineffective Christian "niceness"[3]: true pastoral work is far grittier than this and is vital for a healthy church. It is deliberate work focused both on the prompting of the Spirit and on the ultimate well-being of another. It is not afraid to ask the hard question or remind someone of a hard truth, yet at the same time it is understanding and kind. It is emotionally demanding, intellectually rigorous, and spiritually intense. Such work can be costly for an introvert; it is not a sin for introverts to limit the amount of pastoral work done in a day. Indeed such limits, wisely set, give energy for better quality work which leaves space for emergencies.

In fact, the introvert can be very good at pastoral care precisely because they are inclined towards giving attention to others. They are interested in the inner world of the person, whether that be themselves or others. They engage at a deep level, and this structured listening can come naturally, at least with practice.

Pastoral work need not be gregarious; in fact, considering the constant temptation to please others and serve ourselves, perhaps it ought not be gregarious. We need to listen, and to listen beyond what people actually say: how is it really with the person for whom you are caring? Where are they with God, with themselves, and others? I am always humbled when I have simply listened to someone and they end a lengthy monologue by telling me how helpful I have been to them.

Introvert (public) "worship"

Finally, the most obvious area around which we need to search both for good resources and good practice – and we shall return to the practice in a moment – is the area of public worship.[4] This is where the conversation started for many of us, after all. What sort of resources are there for us to work with, as we seek to engage in "Spirit-filled" worship?

We will discuss the question of liturgy, but I would observe that there are a number of good resources in this field already. Much Anglican material is extremely well crafted and very useful. There are good resources from so-called "Celtic" sources, thinking particularly of the Northumbria Community, as well as Iona and Taizé. There is a lot of good material that has been handed on to us which we can use well.

It is well worth considering questions of "zoned worship". Others have written about this under headings like "liquid worship",[5] which are not specifically written for introverts, but enable us to create space and choice which allow the worshipper to engage in a way which respects choice and the internal journey. It is very possible to find space in a crowd, but thought needs to be given as to how this might be enabled.

If we are serious about wisdom as a spiritual gift, as I have argued, then it is important that we wrestle with questions that reflect the wisdom tradition in the Scriptures. Where does lament fit into worship? How might we search for wisdom together? How do we engage with questioning in a way that builds faith (rather than attacking it), and how do we express faith that goes beyond mere conformity?

These and so many other questions are ones that we need to explore if we are serious about resourcing corporate life which engages and feeds the introvert. Please do join in the discussion online, and, before we end, let's consider some of the dynamics which will be important.

Nine important dynamics in public worship

The public/private partnership

Introverts are often private people and, unsurprisingly, most public worship happens in public. There is an inherent tension here, but it is one to which we are often blind, partly because we are so used to it, but also because much worship is shaped by extroverts, or at least for an extrovert culture.

So, for example, imagine space is given in worship to write things that we want to confess on a piece of paper. This could be perceived as an introvert-friendly activity because it gives worshippers space to process and express themselves individually. However, someone who is a naturally private individual will run a mile before writing down such personal information and then leaving the paper lying around for anyone to pick up. The same discomfort might well be exhibited when it comes to the Anglican practice of "sharing the peace" if someone is in a new or unfamiliar congregation and suddenly everyone starts hugging each other.

None of this is to argue that such public things are wrong, or even that they are unnecessary. It is, rather, the case that allowance needs to be made for those who are uncomfortable "doing their acts of piety in public". Indeed, noticing this also allows us to recall some very clear instructions given by Jesus on this very subject. Matthew chapter 6 does not rule out expressions of worship that are public, but it certainly encourages space for the private.

So, what might one do with the papers in my earlier example? How about giving permission for people to write, or to draw, or simply to imagine the words on the paper? Surprisingly little needs to change to maintain good balance.

Conformity or spaciousness

One of the most common "complaints" I hear from worshippers when we talk about introvert things is that they are fed up with being told what to do.

"Stand up!"

"Sit down!"

"Let's all lift a hand!"

"Shall we give Jesus a rousing round of applause?" (the answer "No!" is not encouraged here)

"Put your arm around your neighbour if you believe Jesus loves them!" This is hard because I do believe Jesus loves them, but I have no idea where they have been! I do, however, notice that their none-too-recent deodorant application has not been sufficient to the challenge set by enthusiastic engagement in worship. I mention this because this is the level to which I am reduced by such instructions. I have absolutely no desire to hug them... but am I withholding a blessing from them? I am now distracted, feeling guilty, and wanting to leave... and just a moment ago I was just as enthusiastic about the Lord as the worship leader was.

Some years ago I was a guest at a large conference with a developed subculture all of its own. After numerous instructions to stand or sit I gave up and stayed seated (it was less embarrassing than staying standing) to allow me to concentrate on what was going on. I ought to say that I was at the back of the auditorium, not on stage, but nevertheless, this was not a move which was understood or appreciated by those around me.

Most of us are willing to do quite a lot in order to participate, but it is essential that those who plan worship realize that not every instruction will be received as gift. To those who are deeply engaged and simply want to focus on Jesus this kind of activity will be a distraction.

What might we do, then? Why not have zones, such that people can be invited to come into these spaces if they want to dance? It's all about permission and encouragement and resisting guilt or wrong compunction.

Time to process and freedom to choose

Both of these elements have been highlighted already in this text, but neither is easy to protect in public worship, especially when it becomes enthusiastic. Preachers know that they get the best response if they ask for an immediate response, and most of us recognize that there are times we need to respond to something immediately in order that we do not let ourselves off the hook.

I remember with great fondness, though, an evangelist who preached his heart out and then by way of asking for a response indicated that those who had not already given their lives to Jesus might be in one of three camps. They might want to walk away, which was absolutely their choice. They might want to invite Jesus into their hearts, in which case they could talk with him, or take his "Two Ways to Journey into Why Jesus" booklet. Alternatively, they might have recognized that there was something important being discussed but they were not sure what they were going to do about it yet. He asked people to pause for a moment and decide what they were going to do next if that was them.

More of this kind of grace-giving space please!

Intimacy within and without

This is a powerful but hidden dynamic which it is really worth considering. Remember that introverts have a lower need for, and toleration of, stimulation. This leads to them feeling the effects of stimulation strongly and in a way which can surprise others who may well have come to think of them as reserved.

One of the ways this plays out is in the whole area of intimacy in worship. The introvert is human with a human need for intimacy. Because the inner life is strong and sustaining, a healthy introvert will create space for intimacy with God and with others in the quiet place. This is life-giving and necessary, and one of the dynamics we need to consider is how we make space for that in public worship.

However, it is also true that when there is public intimacy, this can be quite oppressive for introverts. Many do not really want to be in "group hug" sessions or invited to bear their souls with no notice or preparation time. Public scenes, such as the noises that accompany some charismatic worship, or the use of gifts like tongues in audible worship, will not always come naturally to the introvert. This is more than simply a desire for privacy, though; this is about the place (and nature) of intimacy. Some things are simply better explored within the world in which we are most at home. For the extrovert this may well be external and we need to protect space for that, but somehow that space needs to include those for whom this dynamic is silent and reflective in its expression.

Noise and silence

This conversation is one that might well be expected; however, I suspect we might be going in a direction which is not expected. Many introverts do object to music being too loud, of course, but it is not actually volume which is the general problem. Many of us find that in a typical charismatic noisy venue there is a cocoon-like effect of creating space in the crowd. Everyone is focused on what is happening "up front", and that means that the introvert can be lost in the crowd and alone with Jesus in a way which is counterintuitive. Indeed, this can be a wonderful gift of being able to worship with others in a way which joins us to the whole body and allows space for real engagement.

The question is actually whether space is given for people to inhabit. It is "intrusiveness", not simply volume, which disturbs the introvert's space. Conversely, silence is a wonderful gift, but many people will only be able to cope for a limited period: it is not only extroverts who need to offer their precious gifts with care.

People will have preferences about musical style and the amount of noise, but in each setting the question it would be helpful to have on the agenda is one about whether there can be as much space given as possible between unexpected instructions or changes of mood which will draw the worshipper's attention from the One to whom attention should be given and back to the person with the microphone.

Time and energy

If you are an introvert this will be one of the hardest things to get across to your extrovert friends. For them company is usually energizing; for introverts it is draining. You might love them deeply and really want to be with them, but you will also need time to recharge your batteries. No matter how often this is explained it will always feel to them as if the introvert prefers their own company to that of their friends – as if they are being spurned in some way. Wise introverts will learn to manage this; they will subconsciously prepare for the time that they are going to be with others. It is as if they put an hour's worth of energy into the bank, perhaps with a little to spare, for an hour's meeting... and all is well unless the meeting over-runs.

Of course, for the extroverts over-running is usually fine: it is a joy to be together, and there will be genuine regret if they have to leave to get to something else. Introverts, when they are healthy and refreshed, will cope, but over-running will drain them. When we are already drained, though, whether through tiredness, busyness, stress, or any of a number of factors, this over-running really hurts. This might sound melodramatic but this is the experience that introverts reflect upon when they are kept in meetings: there is a feeling of withdrawal, weariness, sometimes even panic, and it is often in the "over-run" time that bad decisions are made. More than one person has told me that they deal with encounters where they expect extrovert emotional intensity by announcing beforehand that they need to leave half an hour before they actually expect to get away. This enables them to demonstrate that they clearly want to stay, but now they are running late and must dash: this logic is understood both mentally and emotionally in an extrovert world.

These kinds of tricks work, and they are necessary at times, but they are not good ways to love introverts and they cannot be used in more public meetings. Thus clarity about both expectations and discipline in timekeeping really matter.

Liturgy[6] and spontaneity

I find this area really interesting, not least because I grew up thinking that liturgy was almost a dirty word. As I have explored this area of introvert charismatic worship I have come across numerous examples of people finding a deep encounter with the living God in liturgical worship. This has been prevalent enough to make me wonder whether this is authentic introvert charismatic worship.

Certainly, for the introvert charismatic, there are advantages of planned worship, and there are some excellent examples of it out there.[7] When we know what is coming it gives space and time to engage reflectively and immerse ourselves in that which others have prepared carefully for us. Repetition can provide familiarity and the freedom to inhabit an act of worship in a way which releases the attention from worrying about what is coming next and engaging with the One who is the focus of it all.

However, it is easy for anyone to use liturgy as if by rote, and that is no more healthy for introverts than for anyone. Liturgy is a good thing, but it is not the only ingredient in healthy worship. Spontaneity matters, but it does need to be spacious spontaneity if introverts are fully to inhabit it. The tyranny of the latest bright idea is a terrible thing for those who engage by reflecting and then engaging fully. While most of us love giving our extrovert siblings the chance to work out their good ideas we fear being drawn into the mistakes they will make along the way: we make enough of our own.

Internal and external

All of this being said, we do need to remember that the external continues to matter to the introvert. External reference points, in particular, matter and perhaps they matter especially for introverts who won't always have the internal drive to seek them without invitation. Introverts can deceive themselves just as easily as extroverts and I sometimes think that we can do a better job of it. We need challenge and encouragement, and there are times when we just need to stand up and be counted.

Please, then, in all of this, hear the need for wisdom and making the effort to reach out to include introverts. Don't, though, assume that this means allowing us to do everything in the internal space.

The power of permission

Finally, I think the biggest key to this is the giving of permission (which should start young, by the way). There is no way we can shape an act of worship, service, mission, or fellowship that embraces every single person in attendance in a perfect manner. What we can do, though, is give permission to people to engage in a way which enables them to engage rather than doing so in a way which gives the impression that they are engaging. We can do this in many ways, but there are three general ones in my experience.

We need to think about the way we shape the space we inhabit to give people options about how they engage. If a "ministry team" prowls the auditorium looking for people to pray for there is no space for people to engage at their own pace. If, conversely, there are clear invitations given people can choose where they would like to be.

We need to build options into the way we lead and give people permission to respond in a number of ways, without implying that one is the best way and the other is for spiritual wimps. "If God is calling you to the mission field, perhaps you need to respond tonight. You will know if this is a moment of real calling. For some of you it will be really important that you come to the front right now and I will be glad to pray with you. Others need to process this but you also need to respond to God's word – maybe you could come to the front afterwards when others are leaving and talk with one of my team."

We need to build a culture of this in order that the body learns to expect that people will respond differently. The back might love being tickled, the foot might hate it, and both are normal and good.

And, of course, if we get the chance we need to start giving this permission young. Teenage Christians are still teenagers and paradoxically they will be the biggest conformists in the church. They might dress weirdly, like strange music, or giggle in sermons, but when it comes to their peers most of them will hate standing out from the crowd. Those who love and care for introvert teenage Christians have a unique opportunity to give them permission to be themselves in worship from a young age. This might just be the only place in their lives they have this space within which they can be real. This, however, is the subject for another book at another time.

Long ago Elijah found himself in the eye of a storm.[8] We

thought about this in Chapter 3, where we saw him heading for a cave on Mount Moriah, the "mountain of the Lord". Here, alone with God, his life is restored and transformed. Introverts who seek the life of a disciple will find themselves needing these caves, and for me Psalm 40 has become one such place. Here the Psalmist writes:

> I waited patiently for the Lord; He turned to me
>   and heard my cry
> He lifted me out of the slimy pit, out of the mud
>   and mire;
> He set my feet on a rock and gave me a firm place
>   to stand.
> He put a new song in my mouth, a hymn of praise
>   to my God.
> Many will see and fear the Lord and put their trust
>   in him.

If you are introvert and reading this, may this be your experience as you reflect on what we have explored together. The church needs you. The world needs you. Your Lord and God calls you... and does so just as you are.

Notes

Preface

1. See, for instance, the creation account of man and woman and the consequences of the fall. When Adam was created the Lord said, "it is not good for the man to be alone" (Genesis 2:18) and created woman. Post-fall this partnership has turned into desire and domination (3:16).

2. Here and throughout this work I use the word "half" in referring to the division between introverts and extroverts. This is a turn of phrase as statistics seem to imply that about a third of the world is introvert. Interestingly, though, studies seem to show that about two-thirds of Christian leaders are introvert. It would be interesting to see what the statistics were for charismatic leaders.

1. An Introduction

1. New Wine is known mainly for its summer conferences, but actually does many things besides. The summer conferences are large gatherings of thousands of evangelical Christians in the UK who camp on a showground for a week in August, joining together for teaching, ministry, and worship of a fairly enthusiastic and charismatic nature.

2. Susan Cain, in her excellent book *Quiet*, observes that we are all "gloriously complex individuals" with a variety of traits. Some will exhibit both introvert and extrovert traits and can be called "ambivert".

2. What is an Introvert?

1. MBTI aficionados indicate that they don't believe personality types change over a person's life.

2. My correspondent is referring to the five (or possibly four) gifts mentioned in Ephesians 4: pastor, teacher, apostle, prophet, evangelist.

3. http://www.huffingtonpost.com/2013/08/20/introverts-signs-am-i-introverted_n_3721431.html

4. http://gawker.com/15-unmistakable-outrageously-secret-signs-youre-an-ex-1182875137

5. See Chapter 8 of Adam McHugh's *Introverts in the Church*, IVP, 2009.

3. Introversion in the Bible

1. I simply cannot find enough evidence to make valid assertions about any female characters in the Bible. One could argue that Esther shows behaviour typical of an introvert in her dealing with individuals and patient working out of what she thinks. Maybe, though, her planning with Mordecai is an example of extrovert processing. Ruth seems content to work by herself, but the thrust of the book is all communal.

2. The only exception I can think of to this is the company of prophets which we see, for example, around Saul in 1 Samuel 10:5.

3. See Luke 19:1–10 or Luke 7:36–50.

4. I like the cartoon reproduced at http://www.fastcocreate.com/1683402/your-guide-to-interacting-with-an-introvert#1 and the way it expresses this truth.

5. See Deuteronomy 26 for one retelling of this development, from which this phrase is taken.

4. What Do We Mean by "Charismatic"?

1. See Genesis 1 and 2, Psalm 29 (as one example), or John 1 as just a few examples of this in the Bible.

2. See Genesis 3, Romans 1–3, and Psalm 51 for a few biblical examples of this.

3. I could reference the whole Bible, but John 1–3 would not be a bad start here.

4. Consider the Lord's Prayer (Matthew 6:9–13) and Jesus' parting words, Luke 24:49, for example.

5. Charismatics Throughout History

1. If you are interested in this, there are three creeds which have been agreed by Christians and unite us around the world. The simplest is known as the Apostle's Creed. It is in common use in churches with a printed liturgy and reads:

> *I believe in God, the Father almighty,*
> *creator of heaven and earth.*
> *I believe in Jesus Christ, his only Son, our Lord.*
> *He was conceived by the power of the Holy Spirit*
> *and born of the Virgin Mary.*
> *He suffered under Pontius Pilate,*
> *was crucified, died, and was buried.*
> *He descended to the dead.*
> *On the third day he rose again.*
> *He ascended into heaven,*

> *and is seated at the right hand of the Father.*
> *He will come again to judge the living and the dead.*
> *I believe in the Holy Spirit,*
> *the holy catholic Church,*
> *the communion of saints,*
> *the forgiveness of sins,*
> *the resurrection of the body,*
> *and the life everlasting.*
> *Amen.*

2. I remember listening to one famous and popular international charismatic speaker espousing a Christology which shocked me by how far it was from being orthodox and actually had more in common with Charles Gore than Charles Wesley, although I suspect he would be distraught if he were able to see it.

3. Middlemiss, D., *Interpreting Charismatic Experience*, SCM Press, 1996, p. 1.

4. O'Connor, E. (ed.), *Perspectives on Charismatic Renewal*, University of Notre Dame Press, 1975, p. 56.

5. Quoted by Jean Laporte in O'Connor, *Perspectives*, p. 59.

6. Laporte in O'Connor, *Perspectives*, p. 61.

7. Laporte in O'Connor, *Perspectives*, p. 88.

8. Quoted by Laporte in O'Connor, *Perspectives*, p. 90.

9. Laporte in O'Connor, *Perspectives*, pp. 95ff.

10. Cartledge, M., *Encountering the Spirit: The Charismatic Tradition*, Darton, Longman & Todd, 2006, p. 34. Used with permission.

11. Cartledge, *Encountering the Spirit*, p. 35.

12. Laporte in O'Connor, *Perspectives*, p. 62.

13. Bouyer in O'Connor, *Perspectives*, p. 119.

14. Bouyer in O'Connor, *Perspectives*, p. 121.

15. Bouyer in O'Connor, *Perspectives*, p. 123.

16. Cartledge, *Encountering the Spirit*, p. 40.

17. Cartledge, *Encountering the Spirit*, p. 40.

18. Cartledge, *Encountering the Spirit*, p. 42.

19. Cartledge, *Encountering the Spirit*, p. 42.

20. Cartledge, *Encountering the Spirit*, p. 43.

21. A translation of this ancient hymn, taken from www.oremus. org, runs as follows:

> *Bounteous Spirit, ever shedding*
> *Life the world to fill!*
> *Swarms the fruitful globe o'erspreading,*
> *Shoals their ocean pathway threading,*
> *Own Thy quick'ning thrill:*
> *Author of each creature's birth,*
> *Life of life beneath the earth,*
> *Everywhere, O Spirit Blest,*
> *Thou art motion, Thou art rest.*
>
> *Come, Creator! grace bestowing, –*
> *All Thy sevenfold dower!*
> *Come, Thy peace and bounty strowing,*
> *Earth's Renewer! Thine the sowing,*
> *Thine the gladd'ning shower.*
> *Comforter! what joy Thou art*
> *To the blest and faithful heart;*
> *But to man's primeval foe*
> *Uttermost despair and woe.*
>
> *O'er the waters of creation*
> *Moved Thy Wings Divine;*
> *When the world, to animation*

Waking 'neath Thy visitation,
Teem'd with powers benign:
Thou didst man to being call,
Didst restore him from his fall;
Pouring, like the latter rain,
Grace to quicken him again.

Thine the Gospel voices, crying
As with trumpet sound;
Till the world, in darkness lying,
Rose from deathly sleep, descrying
Heavenly light around.
Man, to reach that prize reveal'd,
Arm'd with Thee as with a shield,
Nerved and girt his fight to win,
Quells the prince of death and sin.

Lowliest homage now before Thee
Let the ransom'd pay;
For Thy wondrous gifts adore Thee,
By Thy holiness implore Thee,
While in love they pray:
Holy! Holy! we repeat,
Kneeling at Thy mercy-seat;
There unbosom every woe,
Groanings Thou alone canst know.

Fount of grace for every nation,
Refuge of the soul!
Strengthen Thou each new creation,
With the waters of salvation
Make the guilty whole:
Rule on earth the powers that be;
Give us priests inspired of Thee;
Through Thy Holy Church increase
Purest unity and peace.

Purge and sanctify us wholly
From the leaven of ill;
Save from Satan's grasp unholy;
To a living faith and lowly
Mould the upright will;
Till the olden zeal return,
And with mutual love we burn;
Till in peace, no more to roam,
All the flock be gather'd home.

22. O'Connor, *Perspectives*, pp. 132ff.

23. Middlemiss, *Interpreting Charismatic Experience*, p. 1.

24. Middlemiss, *Interpreting Charismatic Experience*, p. 2.

25. Middlemiss, *Interpreting Charismatic Experience*, pp. 9–29.

26. Harvey Cox, *Fire from Heaven*, De Capo Press, 2001, p. 91.

27. Quote from John Wesley's journal, Saturday 7 July 1739, sourced via http://alaskandreams.net/ekklesia/Wesley%20Quotes.htm.

28. See Kay, W. and Dyer, A., *Pentecostal and Charismatic Studies*, SCM Press, 2004, pp. 1ff.

29. Cartledge, *Encountering the Spirit*, p. 49.

30. The quotations on page 103–106 are taken from Kay and Dyer, *Pentecostal and Charismatic Studies*, pp. 10ff.

31. See Wakefield, G., *The First Pentecostal Anglican: The Life and Legacy of Alexander Boddy*, Grove Books, 2001.

6. Why is the Charismatic World Hard for Introverts?

1. Susan Cain, *Quiet*, Penguin, 2012. Extract from Kindle Edition, p. 29, location 514.

2. I refer the reader both to his published work cited in this text and to his blogs.

3. Cain, *Quiet*, p. 65, loc. 1127.

4. Cain, *Quiet*, p. 66, loc. 1140.

5. Cain, *Quiet*, p. 69, loc. 1192.

6. "The Holy Spirit has long been the Cinderella of the Trinity. The other two sisters may have gone to the theological ball; the Holy Spirit got left behind every time." McGrath A., *Christian Theology*, Blackwell, 1994, p. 240.

7. If you want an excellent read then I would refer you to her book of this title published by Monarch, 2004.

8. Finney, J., *Renewal as a Laboratory for Change*, Grove, 2006.

7. Blessings and Challenges for Charismatics in the Introvert World

1. I am not implying that all charismatic culture is immature, although some parts of it will (and should) be.

8. Why is the Charismatic World Good for Introverts?

1. Look, for example, at the beginning of Luke 9 or Luke 10 and this is the mission that the early disciples were clearly given.

2. Interestingly, one could reverse this reflection for other areas of the church which are dominated by introverts. I think of those I know in monastic life, where the apparent rarity of extroverts make them a wonderful delight to meet.

3. This is a standard formula for a prophet: by way of a random example see Ezekiel 21:1.

4. See, for instance, Luke 4:1, 14, 18.

5. Luke 9, for example, with a repeated pattern in Luke 10.

6. Luke 24:49 or John 16:5–16.

A Letter to Introverts from a Charismatic Among You

1. Susan Cain discusses this and I refer the reader to the quotation reproduced in Chapter 6 (page 116) of this work.

9. What Do Introverts Offer the Charismatic World?

1. See, for instance Luke 4:42.

2. Proverbs presents wisdom as a person, Lady Sophia, as one of my tutors used to call her. Indeed she is almost presented as a person within the Godhead. This may well be part of the theme picked up in John 1 when Christ comes as the "logos", the Word, the verbal expression of God in human form.

Meet Aian

1. This is the study of what a text means in today's context. So with the Bible it refers to the task of asking what God is saying through the text in today's world.

2. This refers to a symbolic act which is often part of Anglican worship on Ash Wednesday at the beginning of Lent. As we enter a season of penitential preparation before we celebrate Easter, worshippers receive the sign of the cross drawn in ash on their foreheads with the words, "Remember that you are dust, and to dust you shall return. Turn away from sin and be faithful to Christ."

10. Six Steps Towards Fullness of Life

1. For instance Leviticus 19:18 picked up in Matthew 19:19.

2. This is a whole new area to be explored. How do you help an introvert child to grow up in a way which is spiritually healthy? Parenting introvert children is clearly as much about protecting and providing space as it is about interacting and stretching.

This is a wonderful and complex balance which deserves a whole lot more exploration.

3. Fry, T. (ed.), *The Rule of St Benedict in English*, The Liturgical Press, 1982, pp. 25–26. The rule of St Benedict is the name given to the instructions that Benedict drew up to govern the life of the monastic communities he established. The "rule" is still followed by Benedictines around the world, and contains much Christian wisdom applicable beyond monastic life.

4. The "shag" is a very popular dance in Carolina (see http://www. youtube.com/watch?v=0usNTJmwk-M for an example). Both of these examples are based on real experience.

11. Towards Some Resources

1. Pippert, R. M., *Out of the Saltshaker and into the World*, IVP, 1994, pp. 121–124.

2. For more information and discussion about this I refer the reader to Grove Booklet 104 in the Evangelism series which I wrote with Nicola David.

3. It is no bad thing to be "nice", but true pastoral work is more than this. This is the visit of an under-shepherd to one of the Master's sheep to care for them. It will involve kindness and care, but it will also entail straight talking, the ministry of prayer, sometimes challenge, sometimes invitation, and deep engagement in the life of another. This is an honour and a privilege, but it is also hard work!

4. I use this phrase in its technical sense, meaning the things that we do when we get together with the intention of worshipping God. This is the Sunday morning service or the celebration, for example, and it is distinguished from the worship that we offer in the rest of our lives.

5. Lomax, T. and Moynagh, M., *Liquid Worship*, Grove, 2004.

6. Here I am using the word liturgy in a slightly lazy sense. I mean worship that has been pre-planned such that people know what they are expecting, often expressed in a printed form of public expression (which is technically called a "rite", of course). This might be classic Anglican styles of worship, or material from the Northumbria Community, but it could equally well be material that has been put together specifically for one act of worship. (If you are interested, the reason this is a lazy use of the word is that the word "liturgy" just means the "stuff" that we do in public worship. Thus there is a liturgy whenever people meet to worship however spontaneous they might think they are.)

7. I refer the reader to the resources online at www.introvertcharismatic.org.

8. See 1 Kings 18 and 19.